Focus in the Age of Distraction

35 tips to focus more and work less

JANE PIPER

Focus in the Age of Distraction

First published in 2018 by

Panoma Press Ltd
48 St Vincent Drive, St Albans, Herts, AL1 5SJ, UK
info@panomapress.com
www.panomapress.com

Book layout by Neil Coe.

Printed on acid-free paper from managed forests.

ISBN 978-1-784521-26-4

The right of Jane Piper to be identified as the author of this work has been asserted in accordance with sections 77 and 78 of the Copyright, Designs and Patents Act 1988.

A CIP catalogue record for this book is available from the British Library.

This book is available online and in bookstores.

Dedication

To all those people who supported and
encouraged me along the way.

Because nobody can do it on their own!

Testimonials

" Out of 35 golden tips, you will find your solution to combine a career AND a happy life."

Sabine Orbello, Holistic Health Coach and Founder of Puricious

" I've read it. I've applied some of the tips. And I've felt the difference right away!"

Katharina Friedemann, Consultant for Stress & Self-Management, Zurich

" Full of useful tips, tricks and techniques to help improve focus where it's needed."

Claire Kowarsky, Online Enforcement Specialist

" As I read Jane's book, many scenarios she describes resonated with me. I found myself evaluating some of the tips and ideas to see if I could incorporate them. That the tips are well summarized and highlighted means I don't have to always remember them. They are quick to find in the book for the moment I need them!"

Sandhya

Acknowledgements

Nobody does it on their own. Without the encouragement and support of many, many people this book would still be a series of blogs. So many people have encouraged me to continue working on this book. A special mention to the beta reviewers (Chris, Sandhya, Claire, Katharina, Montse, Becky and Sabine) who took the time to read the draft, give suggestions and most of all, gave me the encouragement to keep going. And thank you to the people who just said "Wow, that's great, I'd like to read that when it is finished". Small words do count.

Many of the ideas and much of my inspiration has come from people sharing their thoughts, discussing and debating what is happening in their lives, careers and the world today. It is these great conversations, thanks Priscila, Becky, Graham, Chris, Crispen, Vaughan, Vega, Karina and many others, who provided the inspiration for this book.

Most of the anecdotes in this book come from my own experiences working with people, working for people, working in and for companies. These are my view of the events that occurred. Please forgive me if you recognise part of yourself in this book and don't recall the event the same way – we all see our world through our own unique lens.

Many thanks to Isabelle Valera, who had the most amazing ability to capture my thoughts into an illustration.

The final thank you goes to my husband Simon who helped me maintain my work-life boundaries, stress levels and perspective through the days of writing and organising this book.

Contents

INTRODUCTION:

Fast Forward

It's Life, Jim, but not as we know it.

Star Trekkin', The Firm

Are you feeling overworked, overwhelmed and out of control? Are you asking yourself if the world is spinning faster than ever before? There seems to be less time in your day or week. You're always rushing to get things done, jumping from one thing to the next. There is little down-time as you work from early in the morning to late at night.

You're not alone. The world of work has changed significantly in the last five years, and is going to change even more rapidly. But the way we work and how companies organise work has not changed at the same pace. While flexible working, tools and technology are making our work easier, more people are feeling stressed and anxious. Work-related stress and burnout has become a major health issue in many countries with half of Western European employees reporting they consider stress to be common at their workplace and accounting for half of their sick days[1].

Take a trip back in time to 15 or 20 years ago and think about what has changed in the way we work. If you were like me, you had a laptop that was the weight of a baby elephant in comparison to your current laptop. Your mobile phone sent text messages but not email. Remember typing a text message where you had to push a button with a number on it one, two or three times to type in a letter? The word "app" wasn't even in our vocabulary until the first iPhone was launched in 2007[2]. Work was typically done physically at the office, and occasionally at the home office. Can you recall the techno-stress of trying to dial in with a modem? Or plugging in the ethernet cable? There was certainly not the ease of free wifi at every local café.

Along with changes in technology there have been changes in the amount of time and resources available. Things took time and often issues were handled more locally as global headquarters were too far away. The pace of work felt less rushed and less frantic.

I'm not alone in thinking this. When I start my workshops, often I ask the participants to take a trip back in the time machine and think about what has changed in the last 15 to 20 years. Three themes often emerge from the participants: technology, pace of work and global connectedness.

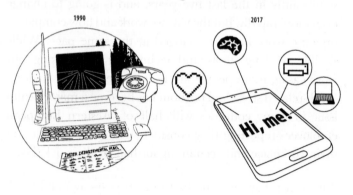

Fast Forward Technology Changes in 30 Years

Unwittingly, these changes have crept up on us, and somehow now we realise we are working more, are more accessible and less in control of our work and personal time. The aim of this book is to give ideas and suggestions of how you can change in the way you choose to work and live so you can optimise your time at work. If you could get just a little bit more done while you were at the office, you could then use this additional time to enjoy life. Imagine if you could save just 30 minutes or an hour a day working. What would that feel like? What would you do with that time – find time to exercise, spend it with your family, work on a personal project or relax and recharge?

But first let's take a trip back in the time machine and see how the world of work and how we react to it has changed and why that leads to stress.

Technology: From 9 to 5 to 24/7

Mobile technology has had a massive impact on our work and life. With smartphones, laptops and wifi available everywhere, nowadays we carry our work in our pocket. We've allowed ourselves to be accessible 24 hours a day, 7 days a week. It is just so convenient in comparison to the technology even five years ago. Now work is always there, right at your fingertips. And this has changed how we feel and cope with work.

Advances in technology have frequently changed our world and the way we work. In the 19th century, the industrial revolution, machines and electricity changed the workforce from craftsmen and farmers to factory workers. Jobs were dull and repetitive with long hours and unsafe conditions in steel mills and textile factories. Mass production was introduced in the early 20th century. Working on an assembly line in a factory became the new way of working. The work remained dull and repetitive but treatment of workers became fairer. The forty hour working week was introduced, health and safety standards improved and various movements from the Kaizen philosophy, continuous improvement to self-managing teams made the work less dull and repetitive.

The march of technological change did not stop. Then came the digital revolution introducing electronics, information technology (IT) and computers. It changed the type of work we did from controlling machines to produce things, to controlling information to produce knowledge. The term *knowledge worker* came about to describe people who work with ideas, concepts and information. They don't produce things that you can actually touch and see. New jobs, levels of management and functions that hadn't existed before in factories came about such as IT, Financial Controlling, Business Systems and Management Consultants.

While the work itself changed fundamentally, the way we think about work hasn't changed. Most offices typically still operate with a forty hour week where you are expected to be physically present. Dividing up work into highly specialised functional areas and into different departments (or silos as they are commonly known) following the mass production model is still the most common form of organisational structure.

In most cases the work is no longer dull and repetitive but busy, demanding and often stressful. There are fewer physical health issues but instead, mental health issues are much more common. Ironically, even though we don't work in a factory, people say they feel like a small cog in a big machine.

The way that we communicate with each other has changed. Email has become the major form of communication and with it, the pure volume of messages that a person receives has exploded, with the average person sending or receiving up to 215 messages per day[3]. And it is not just email: now there is a host of other channels from Instant Messaging and SMS (short message service) to Skype and WhatsApp, among many others. Picking up the telephone or walking across the office to talk to a colleague feels like a social etiquette from a bygone era, just like handwriting and posting a Christmas card. Now we use an SMS to make an appointment to call, no spontaneous phone calls any more.

If you are old enough to know what an inter-office memo is, then you'll know email has two advantages over inter-office memos. But these advantages have now become a disadvantage to us. An inter-office memo took time and effort to print it, envelope it and send it around in the internal post in those brown envelopes. So, people really had to think who the memo was to go to. Once it got in the internal post system, it took time to move around and people took time to respond. Perhaps you'd respond once or twice a day when your secretary put all your correspondence in your in-tray or after you'd collected them from your pigeonhole. In contrast, an email can be copied to many people without any additional effort and is received virtually instantly every minute of the day. As a result, you get many more emails and people expect a response much faster, sometimes instantly.

Despite the speed and ease of email, communication has not improved. Most people still feel they don't know enough about what is going on in their company. More is communicated but less is said. Information may have been sent by email but gets missed because it got "lost in the inbox" or not read properly due to the sheer volume of messages.

And while email may be to blame for information overload inside an organisation, outside the organisation the amount of information available is growing exponentially. Ninety per cent of the data available on the internet has been developed in the last two years[4] . Taking only professional information, there are so many sources of information from Twitter, LinkedIn, YouTube, articles, blogs, online newspapers and newsletters. Then if you include personal channels like Facebook and Instagram, then keeping up with it all is impossible.

Again, the technological ease of publishing online your opinion, research, book or idea without paying for printing or posting means that there is more available, but often of poorer quality. Editors, publishers and marketing departments did play some useful function 20 years ago in limiting quantity and increasing quality.

Information overload leads to feelings of being overwhelmed. You know it is not possible to keep up but there is the pressure of feeling you **should** be keeping up to date in your field and reading (and responding) to every email. Even though it is an impossible task, the "**should**" feeling creates stress and anxiety, a fear of missing out on some important news, information or just not "being there".

Pace of Work

It feels like the world is spinning faster than ever before. The truth is that there are still the same 24 hours a day, 7 days a week and 365 days a year but what we try and pack into these hours has increased. The pace is accelerating as organisations are constantly raising the bar to match competitors and manage new technologies. Organisations, and the people employed by them, face far higher expectations from customers and shareholders as the trust in big corporations has been lost after many scandals and has been replaced with more regulation. A common theme in many businesses is to do more with less and work smarter – but how?

We used to talk about change being a process in an organisation. There were planned and hopefully well-managed projects with workstreams, redesign workshops for processes, organisational structure changes and phased implementation. Now, multiple change programmes are run in parallel, overlapping from one project to another. While one part of the company is acquiring and integrating a new company, the global procurement is centralising purchasing of core products and the finance team is outsourcing its accounting processes to a low-cost country. There is a relentless drive to do things better, faster and more efficiently – which means change.

Time at the top is short with the average CEO lasting just six years in the role[5]. When the CEO changes, the senior management team changes, creating a flow-on effect down the organisation. So just as you get used your boss's quirks, he or she leaves. A new boss comes in with the pressure to perform in his or her first one hundred days, kicking off another cycle of new projects.

All businesses go through cycles of good and bad. When the economy is not good or you are working in a declining industry, then the cost saving programmes start. Just ask someone with a career of over ten years how many cost saving programmes they have been through. I can recall at least five cost saving projects in different companies with names like Project Save, Project King, Project Agile, and the most exciting name, Lighthouse. While the names were different, all used the same blunt tool of a short-term cost savings focus, typically with travel restrictions, hiring freezes, workforce cutbacks, reducing marketing spend and internal budget cuts.

The impact on the people in the organisation was the same whatever the cost saving project was called. New tools, processes and technology were introduced with a view to reducing work, but often ending up, certainly in the short term, creating work. Frustration and stress levels rise when trying to do your job with a smaller budget and fewer resources, or trying to manage globally with travel restrictions.

From the external side, the bar is constantly being raised by customers. Internal and external customers expect fast responses, high standards of service and excellent quality. Competition is fierce in most industries, and keeping up or ahead requires constant updating and upgrading, leading to more change. A company that took over 24 hours to respond to a customer's enquiry would be considered very slow these days.

In a world of constant change, doing more with less and increasing customer expectations, the world is spinning faster to get more and more done in the same amount of time.

Global Connectivity is Shrinking the World

Our world is not only spinning faster but it is also shrinking at the same time. It has never been easier to contact people on the other side of the world though Skype, email and video conferences. We are now all part of one global village, communities interconnected via technology and social media.

Along with the technology to communicate globally, many companies have now designed organisational structures that require more collaboration across the globe, known as a matrix (not to be confused with the sci-fi movie trilogy from 1999 with the same name, but there are some parallels). The typical matrix structure of most large international companies often means that the people you work for, and those you report to, can be widely distributed around the world. You might work in a region or country and have a regional or country manager, but with the matrix, at the same time you are part of another team for your functional area, your product or service line or project. A challenge the matrix brings about is that it increases the number of people who need to be consulted, informed or give their approval. The curse of a matrix structure is global over-collaboration slowing down progress.

There's the joke as the alcoholic pours himself a drink at 8 am in the morning in Europe and says *"...I'm allowed a drink at this time of day, it's 5 pm in Australia..."* Working across multiple time zones can feel like that. There is always somewhere in the world where it is the perfect time to have a meeting, and it is someone else's less than ideal time to meet. To get everyone together on a conference call across three continents, Asia, America and Europe, then someone must take the pain of being available early in the morning or late at night. Or even if you're not scheduled on a call, if you are based in Europe, you arrive at work in the morning with an inbox full of messages from the Asian offices, and end your day with calls and emails coming from America in the evening. The day can get stretched from an early start to a late finish, especially if you keep reading emails on a mobile device after you've left the office. The stress of being globally connected can literally keep us up at night.

The New World of Work

Work has changed from a regular, steady 9 to 5, to a 24/7 connected, fast-paced, constantly changing, information overloaded place. As well as work, the pressure of being the perfect parent, keeping fit, eating well and having an exciting social life can lead to feeling overwhelmed and overburdened.

If you're the typical high achieving mid-career professional with a touch of perfectionism, your standard response to the problem might be to push harder. You try to work longer and try to cram even more into your day and your week. It is a strategy that might even have worked for you in the past. Finally, you hit the wall, feeling exhausted and cynical. You realise this is not making you happy. It is not the career or life you dreamed of, or even close to it. There is not the feeling of "I've made it!" that you expected when you get promoted or land a new project. There are too many times when you feel you've let other people down, from forgetting family birthdays, to losing touch with friends or even times when you just weren't there mentally because you were checking your smartphone for work emails. The mid-life career crisis question comes along – what am I doing it all for?

Work, career, personal and family life all create pressure. These pressures *can* lead to stress and stress *can* lead to burnout. And I deliberately say *can* because it doesn't have to. The tips in this book suggest how you can change the way you choose to work and live. If you could be just a little more productive at work, get more done during the work day, then you'd have time to switch off and enjoy life.

You *Can* Teach an Old Dog New Tricks

I hope you are going to try and apply one or two of the tips in this book, so I have made sure there is evidence so you know that they work. The ideas in this book are based on recent research into neuropsychology and positive psychology, combined with some practical testing in real life with real people.

Neuropsychology's contribution to these ideas is uncovering new understandings of how our brain functions. The single most important neuroscience breakthrough is that you *can* teach an old dog new tricks. The old view of our brain was that it did not grow any more neurons after you reached about 18 years old. It was believed that from 18 years onwards, there was a slow and gradual decline in our mental capacities. You'll be relieved to know however, that we are able to keep developing our cognitive abilities and we can change the way we are thinking at any age[6].

London's black cab drivers became the subjects of a study showing that anyone can continue to grow and develop their brain. Black cab drivers are required to learn by heart all the roads in London without the use of a GPS system. MRI scans of the drivers' brain capacity showed that the area of spatial cognition grew as they studied and practiced [7]. This growth was called neuroplasticity. Despite the big word, it simply means we can train and improve our brain's capacity at any age. It is not too late to teach yourself to concentrate and be more focused.

Positive psychology's contribution to this area is to identify the importance of thoughts and moods on where and how we apply our focus and attention. We all look at the world through our own unique lens shaped by our personality, values and experiences. If we find a job that is aligned with our personality and values then we feel a sense of achievement of doing something that we enjoy, not just working to pay the bills. But even if you're in a job you are not happy with 100% of the time, (hey, who is 100% happy all the time in the real world?) positive psychology puts us in charge of our moods and emotions. We can change our mood to kick out the thoughts and emotions that are distracting us and motivate ourselves to focus on the tasks at hand.

But as well as the science, I've also made sure there is practical proof. Most of these tips I've tried myself. I've also recommended them to my coaching clients and got their feedback after they have tried them. We are human so beware that we are not all the same, and so not everything works for everyone all the time. But one or two of these tips may be enough to help you optimise your attention, get more done and get out of the office sooner.

CHAPTER 1:

Mind Games: Beware of the Sabre-Toothed Tiger

One way to boost our willpower and focus is to manage our distractions instead of letting them manage us.

Daniel Goleman

The human brain is complex but fascinating and often plays tricks with us. Deep focus, undivided attention and intense concentration is not our natural state of being. Our senses are designed to be scanning the environment and looking for potential danger, alert to noises and searching for things out of the corner of our eye that move. Your brain, especially if you are feeling threatened, is rapidly interpreting these inputs from our senses, sorting them into what is safe and what is not. What is not safe needs investigating further. This means we are easily distracted by new stimuli that fires up our senses.

When our enemies were physical (e.g. a sabre-toothed tiger on the savannah or a person from a warring tribe), it was a great survival tactic. And it is still a good survival tactic for physical danger. For example, if you walk out on to the road and suddenly you hear the blast of a horn, you react almost instantly, jumping out of the way of the on-coming car. But today our threats are not so likely to be a physical attack, rather a verbal attack or snide remark from your colleague. When we feel attacked, then we are more easily distracted. Combining this with high stress levels (which we discuss in the next chapter) can put you in a hyper-alert, easily distracted state.

On top of this the modern workplace is full of distractions that bombard our senses. The digital era has developed new ways of distracting us with devices that buzz, beep, bing and sometimes even ring. The trend for open plan office spaces, with the associated noise and close proximity to other people's conversations, can make it extremely difficult to concentrate. Then there are your friendly colleagues who seem to be able to interrupt when you finally get some clear time to think and work. The good news is you can teach yourself how to focus and concentrate better.

Deal With Your Digital Addiction

We have a close personal relationship with our smartphone these days, perhaps a closer relationship than with some of our family. It certainly spends more time at our side than our family, friends or work colleagues. If you've recently lost your phone, you'll know the feeling of panic and loss is as bad as losing your wallet or purse. It's like a part of your brain and life is gone.

The programmes, or apps that run on our smartphones are designed to attract us to interact with them. Many of the apps use the exact same psychological principles that video games and casino gaming machines use to attract and keep your attention. Once you've been drawn into a video game or gambling machine, its aim is to keep you interested as long as possible (so you'll spend more money). It does this by giving you a small, infrequent reward while all the time dangling a big exciting prize at the end. It's the pokie machine where just another spin might bring you the jackpot, or if you keep playing for a few more minutes, then you might be able to catch another Pokemon.

Social media is also designed along the same principles to keep you coming back and staying on the site longer. If you've posted an interesting photo on Facebook, or shared an interesting article on LinkedIn or tweeted a pithy comment, you can watch how many of your friends and followers like it, share it. There is the reward that perhaps it will even go viral. Email on your smartphone or your desk top is similar. The little icon that shows you have new mail draws you in, like a drug addict, to check it immediately. So, we are constantly listening and scanning for those beeps, bings and mail symbols, pulling us away from the deep concentration required for our work.

These short distractions have a surprisingly negative impact on our concentration. Even if your phone is set to mute, just hearing the buzz and without looking at it can destroy your concentration[8]. Stopping to read an email or checking a Facebook post takes you twenty-five minutes[9] to get back to your previous level of concentration. Then it is like a black hole if you do start with just one post or photo on LinkedIn or Facebook. You get sucked into a vortex or a parallel universe and find yourself thirty minutes later still looking at things of highly limited relevance.

To solve this is really very easy:

 Tip 1: Avoid Digital Distraction: Turn off any alerts from your social media and email.

The fastest way to do this for a short period of time, on most smartphones and tablets, is to put it into airplane mode so nothing comes through, and no sound, not even the vibration can be heard. For a more permanent solution, especially with social media, you might wish to choose when you will respond, so you can change the settings permanently so that you don't receive alerts.

Overwhelming Open Plan Office Spaces

The days of long rows of offices like tiny rabbit hutches has gone, probably for the better when it comes to light, space and building connections with your colleagues. However, the open plan office with a desk in an open floor is not designed to help you concentrate. There are other people talking, and even if their conversations are not involving you, it is still hard not to listen, especially if it is an interesting topic. There is a general noise level and people constantly coming and going. Just being polite enough to say hello to people in the morning and goodbye as people leave in the evening means short interruptions for the first and last hour of the day.

It is interesting to note how the different teams in a floor space settle into a different level of acceptable noise and distraction. I worked on a project of implementing a new computer system and two teams were divided across the floor with a corridor in between. On one side, there were the computer programmers where they worked in church-like silence, concentrating intensely on their work, usually with their headphones on. They worked on quite separate tasks and quick discussions happened in hushed tones so as not to disturb others.

On the other side of the floor, where I sat, was the Change Management team. We were looking at the implications of the processes redesign on people, their work and organisation. There were constantly conversations whirling around, informal meetings taking place, excited discussions where everyone would suddenly be involved in topics (sometimes topics of limited relevance to work). It was good for teamwork, sharing information and often a lot of fun. But it was very difficult to concentrate on a detailed task.

There was quite a difference in the personalities between the two groups, our team mostly chatty extroverts, the programmers quiet introverted types. Sometimes you can learn from the opposite personality trait. I borrowed an idea from the programmers' side. When I needed to concentrate on a task, I'd put on my headphones and listen to some music while working. The headphones helped me to not hear the noise but mostly helped me to avoid getting sucked into listening or contributing (usually uninvited) to a conversation. The headphones were also effective in signalling to others that I was working on a more intense task. Other team members would tend not to interrupt as often or even move their conversation out of the open space area.

Tip 2: When you don't work in a quiet space, create your own quiet zone by using headphones with either white noise or music

For some people, working while listening to music or the radio is distracting (see Chapter 3 for the debate on whether music helps your concentration) but even the act of putting on headphones can be enough to get into the zone and avoid interruptions. If all else fails, you can play some white noise that cancels out other sounds[10].

Irritating Interruptions

The older style of office and the stiff hierarchy often prevented people from being interrupted. The closed office door was always a signal not to interrupt. Senior managers and executives had secretaries posted close to their door, who you had to ask permission of before you could just tread the hallowed carpet of their office. Along with open plan space came the open-door policy and a flatter hierarchy; trying to be an approachable leader can mean that people feel they can approach you at any time. I'm sure nobody would want to go back to a stiff, awkward, unapproachable style of leadership but we do need to find a way to balance this with being constantly interrupted.

I had one coaching client who was a global account manager so his job required a significant amount of travel. When he was finally back in the office, he'd have a lot of work to catch up on. It would have been the first time that his team had seen him for several weeks and issues had been building up while he was away. He got very frustrated when needing to concentrate, say to get a presentation done, that there would be one interruption after another from his team members.

He didn't want to be some remote and distant manager that his team could not approach, but at the same time it was necessary to have time to work in a concentrated way. We discussed several different ways to handle this issue and came up with a couple of strategies that worked and suited his style. One was to schedule a meeting one-on-one with each of his team bi-weekly. He'd try to do it by phone if he was travelling. This meant urgent issues that couldn't wait would be covered in this meeting, not saved up for when he was back in the office. The second action was to have a discussion with the team about the issue of approachability but also getting work done. The team agreed they also had a similar problem of finding uninterrupted time to concentrate on detailed tasks. They agreed they could all schedule in their diary a space of two blocks of two hours a week where they could work uninterrupted. While four hours a week was not much, the discussion with the team raised the awareness of frequent interruptions, which seemed to limit these disturbances.

Some offices have taken this to an extreme by setting up red and green lights on their employees' desks to indicate when you can interrupt someone or not. The FlowLight[11] shows red when the person is actively clicking their mouse and typing, green when not. Two things concern me about this solution. Firstly, it isn't the person in control but the machine. The person doesn't decide when they need to concentrate but the software does, based on keystrokes and clicks. It takes away your control: being in control is important to feeling positive and energised. Secondly, it equates concentration with how quickly the person is working on the computer. Sometimes it is just as important not to interrupt thinking as keystrokes and mouse clicks.

And conversely, you could be rapidly clicking while surfing the internet or scrolling through Facebook postings.

An answer simpler than complex technology would be to discuss within your team and agree the norms that you all work to in order to find some time to concentrate on bigger projects each week and avoid interruptions. It may become the standard way of working in your team, optimising the work performance for everyone.

 Tip 3: Agree some norms in your team of how you can have some uninterrupted chunks of time to concentrate on your work.

Mindlessly Multitasking

Confession time – we've all done it. I'm sitting in a teleconference, I put the phone on mute and start typing away, just answering a few emails, nothing requiring too much thought. I'm listening to the teleconference with half an ear, then suddenly there is a voice asking, "Jane, are you there – can you answer this question please?" Suddenly I realise that I am no longer listening to the conference call. Caught out multitasking! Like the rabbit in the headlights, stuttering to find something to say.

Multitasking is when we try and do several things at the same time. Multitasking is the greatest myth of the modern world of work. Everyone thinks they are the greatest multitasker, that by multitasking they are getting things done faster. In fact, you are rapidly shifting between two or three tasks and these shifts consume mental energy and decrease concentration on the task at hand.

Try this simple demonstration of multitasking. Get a watch or your phone and set the timer. Count as fast as you can out loud from 1 to 10. See how long that takes you (about 3 seconds probably). Now do the same exercise but say the first 10 letters of the alphabet, from A to J (again about 3 seconds). Now try going 1A, 2B and so on and see how long it takes you. My guess is it takes you more than twice as long, probably about 15 seconds. Two simple tasks that if you try to multitask, take you more time than doing either separately.

I can hear you saying *"...but that is a silly example because it is just practice on the first two tasks that makes them faster, and you could practice being just as fast on the 1A, 2B exercise...".* Yes, you could practice so that it becomes as automated a task as counting and saying the alphabet. And if you have one task that is very automated, with the other less automated, it might be possible to do both together. For example, if you are an experienced driver, you can drive a car along a motorway and at the same time talk to the person next to you or listen to the news on the radio. However, when you get into a built-up area and you are trying to navigate your way around an unknown place, then you'll notice that you might turn off the radio or stop talking so you can concentrate, or pull over to the side of the road to read a map or programme your GPS. You can do some very automated tasks, talking and driving but not more complicated ones. For this reason, most countries ban texting and reading your phone while driving.

If you still don't believe me, then try this. Go out for a walk, somewhere you can go at a steady pace. Start to do some complicated mathematic sums, like starting with 2879 subtracting 47, then from this total then subtract 46, and this total 45 etc. See if you notice that you have started walking more slowly. Even an automated task we know well like walking is hard to multitask.

Multitasking should be defined as fast-switching between tasks. Our brains are not actually processing two things at the same time but switching quickly between the two (or three or four) tasks. We have a limited capacity to process information and problem solve. If a task is automated it takes less effort to do (like counting or driving) and it is easier to switch almost instantaneously between the two tasks so it seems like you are doing both at once. To process complex problems, or write a well-worded email, or to listen to the content of a conference call or to hold a difficult conversation (not just chat to the person next to you while driving), requires concentrating on that one task. Jumping between tasks, we lose our train of thought and it takes time to bring the brain back to the topic.

Multitasking Madness

So why do we feel that we are achieving more when we multitask? Imagine you're in a conference call, and let's be honest the topic is a little dull, a bleep on your phone – it's an email. You can answer it now, the person who sent you a mail will be happy with your fast response. And we are more and more conditioned by others' expectations to answer that text or email immediately. There is an immediate reward by responding to the email but not much from the dull teleconference. Perhaps in the long term there might be some pain in that you missed some information that is relevant for some future event. The worst example of multitasking on a teleconference I heard about, was a guy doing two teleconferences simultaneously!

One of the very persistent myths is that women are better at multitasking than men. I believe it comes from a traditional view around gender roles. It gets propagated in jokes about men not being able to undertake household chores while watching sport on television. If anyone, male or female, is doing a household chore, such as stirring a pot of soup or emptying the dishwasher, then it is possible to also do something else as well, e.g. hold a conversation or read a recipe for the next step. The one task is routine and automated so you can do another automated task besides. But finding reliable scientific evidence to prove women are better at multitasking on work-related tasks is much less clear [12]. Women might choose to multitask more often than men and therefore be more practiced at it. But in a work context, multitasking is not helpful for your concentration, whatever your gender.

Multitasking has another downside – it leads to a lot of not quite finished tasks. It is easy to be working on multiple things. How many screens do you have open at one time when you are working on your computer? Have you finished the things that you were doing on each of the programmes, saved and closed it? Or do you get to the end of the day and find a presentation that is only partly done, or a spreadsheet that you haven't quite finished as you jumped to another topic. It is easier to overlook something if you were doing several things at once. After an interruption, if you are able to jump back to the one task that you were doing before, then it's fine; if you try and jump back to the three or four tasks that you were doing, you will probably miss one.

 Tip 4: Avoid multitasking: Research shows if you concentrate and focus on one task at a time, you will be able to complete it faster. Prioritise and complete one task after the other.

Create Your Zone of Concentration

In the era of fake news and urban myths you shouldn't believe everything you read. When it comes to facts about people's attention span, the myth that is often quoted is that our attention span is now shorter than that of a goldfish. A goldfish is said to have an attention span of about twelve seconds and humans have an attention span of only eight seconds these days. You'll be much relieved to know that this is complete rubbish.

The study often cited referring to the eight second attention span was conducted by Microsoft in Canada, and measured the average time that a person spends reading a webpage on the internet[13]. Now you can see where the myth began. Your attention span is not simply the time you spend reading a webpage. The time that you spend reading a webpage has little to do with your ability to pay attention and more to do with the fact that you are skim reading to check for the relevance of the website before reading closely. If your attention span was only eight seconds, then you wouldn't even be able to complete a sentence that you just started (though I must admit this happens to me on some occasions!).

And while we are correcting myths, no one is sure how long the attention span of a goldfish is either. How can you measure a goldfish's attention span?

So, what is the average person's attention span? The answer is like one you'd get from a lawyer – "it depends". If you are highly motivated and engaged in the task or topic, then you can concentrate on it for a longer period than if you are not interested. If you find the topic boring or the task not very challenging, then you are more easily distracted. Think about movies. The one you find really interesting and are engrossed in, then time just flies by without you noticing. A movie you're not very interested in, you find you are constantly looking at your watch, fidgeting in the seat because it is uncomfortable and wondering when it will end.

To get a more precise answer to how long is the average attention span than "it depends", then around 20 to 30 minutes is a frequently quoted number. And with some training, the right motivation and level of interest, you can concentrate for much longer, up to 50 minutes.

You can train yourself to concentrate better. One technique that has been around for many years is called the Pomodoro technique. This technique is named after the Italian word for tomato as the person who developed it used a kitchen timer shaped like a tomato. My suggestion is a more modern version using your smartphone as the timer, so I call it the Airplane Mode Technique.

The technique is simple: you set your smartphone timer for 25 minutes and focus solely on your task for these 25 minutes. The trick with using your smartphone is to put it into airplane mode at the same time so the bings and bleeps from your email and Facebook don't distract you. When the alarm goes off, give yourself a 5 to 10 minute "mind break" to daydream, get a coffee, go for a walk. Then get back into it for another 25 minutes of concentrated work. As you develop the skill of focussing without distraction, you can set your timer for longer.

Airplane Mode Technique

1. Limit your distractions: turn off all the notifications on your phone. The easiest way is to put it into airplane mode. Turn off your email and other PC screen alerts.

2. Set the timer (on your phone or another timer) for 25 to 50 minutes.

3. Try to focus and concentrate on just one task or topic.

4. After 25 to 50 minutes, stop and take a real break of 5 to 10 minutes.

5. Think of the progress that you've made – small steps towards a bigger project.

6. Repeat.

AIRPLANE MODE
Technique

Limit your distractions

1

Turn off all the notifications on your phone. The easiest is to put it into airplane mode. Turn off your email and other screen alerts.

2

Set the timer for 25 to 50 minutes.

3

'To Do'

ONE Task

Try to focus and concentrate on just one task or topic.

4

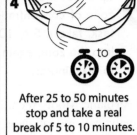

After 25 to 50 minutes stop and take a real break of 5 to 10 minutes.

5

Think of the progress that you've made – small steps on the way to a bigger project.

6

REPEAT

Repeat

Repeat

Repeat

Repeat

Airplane Mode Technique

While the Pomodoro technique has been around for years, more recently, evidence using apps that track a person's working style have shown how effective it is. The Dragnium Group measured productivity levels in relation to working hours. The most productive people were those who took regular breaks; the average in their study was 52 minutes working with a 17 minutes break. While working, they were 100% dedicated to the task, no quick check of Facebook or email. They also took a real rest during the break, a short walk or a chat – something away from the desk[14]. While the 52 minutes work and 17 minutes break seems a little too precise, the general rule of 50 minutes on and 10 minutes off works well too.

 Tip 5: Use the Airplane Mode Technique to create a zone of concentration for 25 to 50 minutes on a task, take a 5 to 10 minutes break, and then get into the zone again, concentrating for another 25 to 50 minutes.

The Airplane Mode Technique is great for concentrating on analytical and analysis tasks. For creative tasks and coming up with new ideas then almost the opposite applies. You need to un-focus and let your mind wander freely. In a positive daydream (not running over the past with guilty thoughts) we are playful, imaginative and very creative. For example, when you are preparing a presentation and trying to think about how to make the key message interesting to the audience, imagining yourself as one of them can be a very useful trick to help you understand the audience. Or by allowing your mind to wander to different areas, it picks up thoughts from different domains which, when applied to a new area, can become a creative idea.

Declutter Your Headspace

If you've now found time to concentrate, how do you keep yourself focused instead of your mind wandering off to another topic? Often it seems we try to hold too much information in our heads and then something gets forgotten. Our brains are well suited to creating ideas, but not remembering those ideas, figures or facts. We have a working memory where we briefly hold facts, figures or ideas. Most of us can hold between 4 and 7 pieces of information at one time, and you can train yourself to improve your memory. The World Memory Champion Alex Mullens memorised 500 digits in 60 seconds[15] . But if you are not even close to being a World Memory Champion, you'll forget stuff quite easily. If we want something to go from our short-term memory to our long-term memory, like a phone number, we need to memorise it by repeating it. But then it doesn't just pop back into our mind, we need a context to recall it.

So, accept that you are going to forget things and write them down. You're sitting at your desk working and suddenly the thought pops into your head that you must remember to pick up milk on the way home from work tonight. You keep saying to yourself "I must remember to pick up milk", hoping to commit it to memory. Instead the thought takes away some of your mental capacity and becomes a distraction. Write it down, stick the note where you'll see it close to your bag, coat or car keys. Then the thought can be forgotten for the rest of the working day. At the end of the day when travelling home, hopefully it is fresh in your mind and you won't forget the milk.

It also works if you are in your "zone of concentration" described in Tip 5 with the Airplane Mode Technique.

If you are in the middle of preparing a presentation and suddenly remember that you meant to send an invitation for the meeting that you are planning next week, write yourself a note and get back on task. Don't interrupt your period of concentration.

A checklist is a great way of decluttering your headspace. For me, routine is boring. I love change and variety. But boring routines help by automating our actions and meaning we use less mental energy. So, I've learnt to do boring routines, but only the hard way, because I've forgotten something. I travelled frequently for business and so often forgot things that made my trip a complete pain. From packing an adapter plug for the overseas power sockets, sunglasses when leaving Zürich in winter and going to the Middle East, or taking an umbrella to the UK. One time I left my passport at home and only realised when I got to the airport. I was early for the flight and fortunately live only 20 minutes from the airport. I grabbed a taxi which drove me at breakneck speed to and from the terminal. Then I ran to security, begging people in the queue if I could jump in front of them and arriving at the gate as they were calling through the loudspeaker for me to board as the gate was closing. Never again! After that I developed my business travel checklist to double-check after packing.

Similarly, for a monthly management report where the data came from several different IT systems, I once had to write down the steps so my deputy could do it while I was away on a long holiday. Once I was back and doing it myself, I realised it was extremely useful to be able to just think about the information, and not to be concentrating on the steps that it took to create the report. An automated routine helps save the mental energy for what matters.

Tip 6: Declutter your headspace by creating lists of routines and write down reminders and ideas as they pop into your head.

Saving mental energy is also important at the emotional level. How many times have you been thinking back on a difficult conversation and then said to yourself *"…I wish I'd said this…"* or *"…I should have said that…"*? You're replaying the conversation over and over again in your mind. On one side, we might have limited capacity to remember facts, on the other side our brain is good at recalling an emotionally charged event (though often twisting the scene each time).

An argument with your partner before work or a painful discussion with a difficult customer can keep repeating in your mind like a song stuck on replay. Psychologists call this ruminating. Ruminating drains the mental energy that you could use to focus and concentrate on your current work. It can also keep building up more emotions, such as blaming yourself for not having handled the conversation well.

If you are a person who tends to ruminate, then here are a couple of tips to help. Reflection is a great tool to help you learn, looking back over an event and thinking "What would I do differently next time?" It can help to write out the issue in a journal. Committing the issue to paper can give you the feeling that it is now out; write down the lessons you've learned and then put it aside. You are less likely to replay it repeatedly.

Likewise, talking to the right person (someone who will empathically listen and not try to blame you or the other person) can be helpful in the same way if you both work on what could be done differently next time. In the next chapter, we look at meditation and mindfulness as two techniques to help put some mental distance between you and the issue.

 Tip 7: Don't waste your mental energy by ruminating on things that you can't do much about. If you do find yourself ruminating, write down your thoughts in a journal or discuss the issue with someone.

Focus and Get More Done

With knowledge work, getting more done doesn't mean working longer hours. Our jobs require mental sharpness and thinking. The ability to analyse and assess information, come up with solutions to complex problems and present a convincing argument, requires deeper concentration, not more time sitting at the desk. So, train yourself to concentrate and work in a focused way. If you do keep the focus, avoid distractions and keep away the energy-draining thoughts, then you'll be sharper, more insightful, more able to solve problems and be creative – all the skills we need to be successful in this knowledge age.

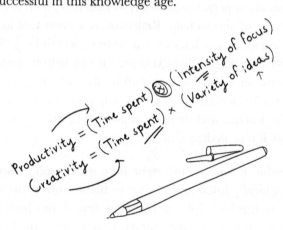

Productivity and Creativity

Chapter Recap

1. *Avoid Digital Distraction: Turn off any alerts from your social media and email.*

2. *When you don't work in a quiet space, create your own quiet zone by using headphones with either white noise or music.*

3. *Agree some norms in your team of how you can have some uninterrupted chunks of time to concentrate on your work.*

4. *Avoid multitasking: Research shows if you concentrate and focus on one task at a time you will be able to complete it faster. Prioritise and complete one task after the other.*

5. *Use the Airplane Mode Technique to create a zone of concentration for 25 to 50 minutes on a task, take a 5 to 10 minutes break, and then get into the zone again, concentrating for another 25 to 50 minutes.*

6. *Declutter your headspace by creating lists of routines and write down reminders and ideas as they pop into your head.*

7. *Don't waste your mental energy by ruminating on things that you can't do much about. If you do find yourself ruminating, write down your thoughts in a journal or discuss the issue with someone.*

CHAPTER 2:

Sttress Makes You Stupid

Did you ever stop to think,
and forget to start again?

Winnie-the-Pooh, A.A. Milne

I'm so stressed out that I can't think straight! It can feel like you're going crazy, forgetting important things, not able to see simple solutions when you are so busy. You're rapidly jumping from one task to the next to get things done faster, planning the next task or thinking about the next meeting while you are trying to complete the current task, all as fast as possible. In the haste, rush and stress, it seems that the mind is scrambling to keep up. I remember feeling awful when I forgot my mother's birthday in the rush to get some work finished and things done before going on holiday. It suddenly made me realise how stressed I was, forgetting the important things in life.

When we are stressed we are in effect stupid. Neuroscience shows how the stressed brain is less effective in processing information, solving problems[16], and more likely to forget things[17]. The most advanced part of the brain, called the prefrontal cortex, is where our "executive functions" take place. This is the area of the brain that helps us manage our social interactions, come up with creative ideas and solve complex problems. There are many biological processes that our bodies go through during stress, that also impact our brain functioning. So, unless you manage your stress levels, your mental performance will be below your best.

One Person's Stress, Another Person's Challenge

One of the areas around stress that continues to surprise me is the fact that if you put two or three people together in the same situation, with the same demands and the same pressure, one person can feel very stressed and the other person is not at all bothered. Individual differences in dealing with stress was something I came across early in my career when an Executive Assistant named Helen came and spoke to me about how stressed she was feeling. Helen had been given more executives to support, was making mistakes and was worried she would not be able to meet everyone's expectations.

While I was listening to her, my first reaction was "You're stressed; imagine if you had your boss's job! He has to make decisions on multi-million-dollar investments and operations". Fortunately, I didn't say this out loud and just listened. I began to understand that how we deal with stress is often more important than how stressful the situation is. In Helen's case, she was very focused on making sure every detail was correct for the people she supported. She was a perfectionist, which was partly what made her an excellent assistant. But her anxiety about working for more people and a concern that she'd make more mistakes was rising. Her stress was very genuine, even if the mistakes she made didn't have company-wide implications like her boss's job.

How we each deal with stress is a complex mix of factors of our personality, our upbringing, our previous experiences with coping with stress, our style of thinking, and even possibly our physiology[18]. As our brain and body are so closely connected, then physical reactions can have a huge impact on our feelings about stress. At our workplace, the leadership style and the organisational culture (more in Chapter 7) also have a huge impact on managing work-related stress. The level of stress that we feel at work can be impacted by what else is happening in our life.

As in Helen's case, how we choose to interpret an event makes a difference to whether it is stressful or not. The good news is if we can change how we think about stress then we are able to manage stress better.

To understand stress, we need to understand the difference between stress and pressure, and take a little excursion into understanding what is going on in our bodies when we feel stressed. Pressure is the actual event that occurs, or may occur in the future. It is the demand placed on you. Stress is your reaction to the pressure, how you feel, and ranging from overloaded to burnout.

INVERTED U OF STRESS

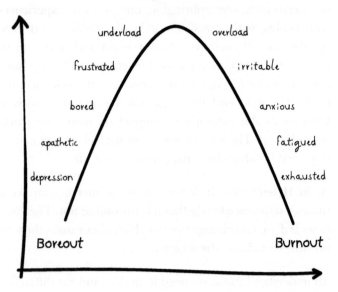

Optimal Stress Levels *(by Yerkes and Dodson)*

There is an optimal amount of pressure that creates enough challenge for you so you feel engaged and interested in the things you are doing. Like when you are excited to be learning something new, or really concentrating, preparing an important presentation or studying for an exam. Too much pressure, rather than making you feel stimulated and challenged, can make you start to feel overwhelmed and worried whether you can achieve the goal. The thoughts become more negative, leading to anxiety and exhaustion.

At the far end of extreme stress levels is burnout. I'm often asked by people who are feeling stressed, and have been feeling that way for a while, if they are burnt out. The difference between stress and burnout is in three main areas[19]. Firstly, people feel overwhelmed physically as well as being emotionally exhausted. They can't switch this feeling off even if they take a vacation and get some rest. Secondly, they are very cynical and disengaged with their job. They no longer feel a sense of purpose or excitement in what they are doing. Finally, they start to question their competence and ability to do their job.

Definition of Burnout

1. Physically and mentally exhausted, even after time to rest and recover.

2. Disengaged and cynical about their profession and organisation.

3. No sense of accomplishment or pleasure in what they are doing. Feeling that everything is hopeless[20].

Often it is other people, colleagues, family and friends that notice someone is not "himself" or "herself". They are working long hours but making many mistakes, or repeating things like sending the same question in an email two or three times. They are missing the obvious things that they used to be able to do well, like spot a mistake in a financial statement, or handle a challenging conversation. At the later stages of burnout, physical exhaustion can lead to collapse where people feel they can't get out of bed or do anything.

Stress, on the other hand, might cause you to feel tired but after some time to recover (like a vacation) your energy returns. A stressed person can still find meaning in what they are doing and feel like they are achieving something, just they have too much to do.

People often use the word burnout to describe a time when they have felt very stressed. Frequently it is used to explain why someone has quit their job and taken a new career direction. This probably isn't a burnout in the sense of the definition above. Adding to the confusion, in some countries burnout is a recognised medical condition, but in other countries it is not. Burnout is a serious condition and beyond what this book can deal with. It requires personalised advice from professionals like doctors, psychologists, therapists. The advice in this book to help people to deal with stress before it reaches burnout stage.

On the opposite side, too little stress can lead to boredom, frustration and in the worst case, depression, known as bore-out. A manager in France sued his employer for bore-out after they took away all his managerial duties and left him with what he described as mind-numbingly boring tasks for four years. He claimed that it was "...*an insidious descent into hell, a nightmare...*" that led to him suffering from health problems, including epilepsy, ulcers, sleep problems and serious depression[21]. Apart from our unfortunate Frenchman, cases of bore-out are relatively rare.

Too much pressure or too little is not good for us physically or mentally. We are all unique and we react differently to the same pressure. One person's stress is another person's challenge. Imagine extreme sports like skydiving, base jumping or free solo climbing (rock climbing without ropes, harness and protection). For the rare breed, they find this totally exhilarating. For (most) other people, they find it frightening and for some, even the thought of skydiving could bring on extreme anxiety.

To understand how we can deal with stress, it is important to understand the physical and psychological symptoms so you can recognise stress, and then you can work on how to change your reaction.

The Physical Side of Stress

Let's go back to our example where you step out to cross a road and suddenly a car horn blares at you. You will automatically jump out of the way. At the same time, your heart will be beating like crazy, you'll be breathing very fast and you might feel a throbbing or pulsing of blood in your head. What you can't feel is that this automatic response has also been sending blood to your muscles and away from other parts of the body where it is not as needed, like the stomach (butterflies in the stomach). Your pupils will dilate, your perspiration will increase, (clammy hands), tears and digestive secretions will reduce, (dry mouth). All this happens so you are ready to attack (fight) or get out of the way of danger (flight) – so called the fight or flight response[22].

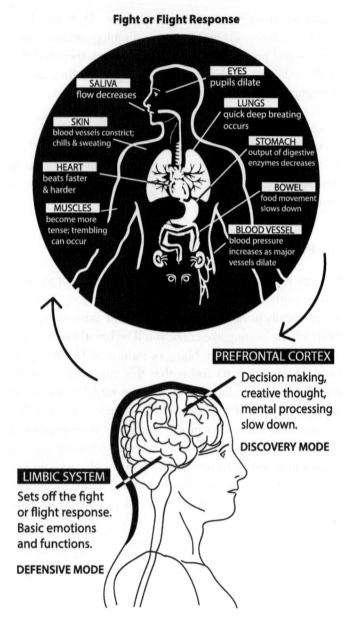

Fight and Flight Response

Inside your body what you also can't see but will feel the effects of, is that adrenaline and nor-adrenaline is being released. Cortisol is released, increasing your blood pressure, mobilising energy (glucose and fats) and reducing the white blood cells that fight bacteria. Two other chemicals are released that help increase your blood pressure (oxytocin and vasopressin) and blood sugar is increased to give you more fuel. In the case of a car potentially running you over, your body is prepared for the response to flee the situation.

After an incident, like jumping out of the way of an oncoming car, your body will slowly return to normal, your parasympathetic nervous system takes over, helping you relax and your nervous system returns to a normal state. This sort of event would be described as an acute stress incident. This fight or flight response is perfectly tuned for ensuring that you avoid danger. Adrenaline has enabled people to manage to hobble several miles for help after they have broken an ankle. A small amount of this stress can help us physically to perform better in a race or competition.

In our modern world, most of the dangers we face are not things that can be solved by attacking physically or running away. Unlike where our ancestors were involved, our life is not being threatened by a sabre-toothed tiger on the savannah. Attacking or fleeing were good options under those circumstances. The world has changed rapidly in a few thousand years but our physical makeup has not changed at the same pace. Instead we are now threatened by poor performance reviews, the anxiety of presenting in front of a large audience, being criticised during a meeting or being gossiped about behind our back.

Our body's automatic reactions do nothing to help us in these situations. When these physical responses are regularly triggered over a long period of time, as there is no release to bring the body back to normal, it leads to long-term effects on our health. This is called the chronic stress response to constant and persistent stress over a long period of time. The symptoms like high blood pressure, heart palpitations, irritable stomach and bowel and a poor immune system can be a result of reactions to chronic stress. These have long-term negative impacts on your health.

The Psychological Side of Stress

Like the story about what happens in your body when you are stressed, stress can be both beneficial and a hindrance to your ability to think, concentrate and recall things. If you are trying to do complex reasoning, like mental arithmetic, then some stress will help you go faster. But the flip side is that you make more mistakes because you work faster and will be less accurate. You're suddenly surprised when you look back at some work you were doing and see a mistake that is so obvious and something you can normally do well; you can't believe that you didn't notice it[23].

Creative problem-solving is not enhanced by stress. The more stressed you are then the less likely the connections in different parts of the brain are working together to bring about those "A-ha" moments and bright ideas. It is why when people are very stressed, they seem unable to see what appears to be obvious solutions to the people looking from outside.

Stress likewise has positive and negative impacts on our memory. Nearly anyone can recall where they were when they found out Princess Diana had died, or when they first heard about the 9/11 attacks. Our minds are often able to recall negative events very clearly. This is an adaptive response so that we would learn to avoid a negative event again. For example, to recall that this was the place where a hungry lion lives was a wonderfully helpful memory in former times!

On the flip side, memorising facts, figures and events, like when you swot for an exam, high stress levels are not helpful as it makes it harder to transfer information into your long-term memory. Stress also has more impact on your spatial memory, meaning that you forget where you left things like your keys or handbag. The increased levels of cortisol have a big part to play in influencing the ability to lay down and recall memories. [24]

Stress can help to focus and concentrate on the negative issue that is causing you stress. If you see a threat, let's take our hungry lion again, when you meet him then the stress response will help you focus very intently on what the lion is doing to help you avoid danger. Everything else will be out of focus and you will ignore things that are not important in this situation. This is clearly a helpful adaptive behaviour. Again, this reaction is not so useful with modern day stresses. A negative event like a less-than-positive interaction with a colleague, will be what you end up focusing on, rather than the report in front of you that needs to get done by the end of the day[25].

Stress and Bad Behaviour

Stress generally has a negative impact on your emotional intelligence. In situations where things don't normally worry you, when you're highly stressed you more easily become irritable, snappy and agitated. It can be that the same situations bring out the worst behaviour in you. Normally the commute to work is a neutral event. It's not exactly fun but it is not that bad. On a day you are feeling stressed, then it seems that every other idiot driver is on the road, or every second person on public transport is talking too loudly, smells bad or has too large a bag.

This general level of irritation leads you to be more impatient, abrupt or even rude. Not thinking before you say something can lead to an emotional outburst, often taken out on the wrong person. In the end, it's you who is the person that no one wants to work with. Like the Financial Controller Alexia that we all used to tip-toe around in the office as she was prone to emotional outbursts. Alexia was hard-working and dedicated. Working in finance there were times when the pressure was on, like at year-end closing. When the stress increased, her reaction when you asked a legitimate question was to rant at you. Conversations went like this:

> Q: "Excuse me Alexia, can I bother you with a quick question?"

> A: "…You know I am very busy with these reports that Mark asked for on the closure in China. I just don't understand: one minute we are investing in Asia, now we are shutting this operation in China. This company doesn't know what it is doing. And look, look at this! The Financial Controller in China has sent a spreadsheet to me without the date and confidential in the footer…"

Eventually you might get to ask your question, but next time you probably tried to find someone else to answer it. Alexia's response was a typically aggressive one. The stress led to anger, not at you personally, though you were the one who got to hear about it. At times when the pressure wasn't high she was perfectly capable of controlling her emotions and answering a simple question, in fact, being quite helpful.

The opposite of taking out the stress in an aggressive way is by becoming more passive. Withdrawing from the situation and social contact. For example, taking more days off sick from work to avoid the situation. One of my clients who was finding work very stressful, stopped answering the phone, although she still answered emails. It was a form of passive withdrawal away from colleagues who were demanding and difficult at a time when she felt she didn't have the emotional resources to cope. By email, she had time to think of an answer. When things got more stressful, she would retreat from the work space to walk up and down the stairs, carrying some papers to make it look like she was going to a meeting.

Ongoing stress leads people to look for ways to manage stress in ways that might make them feel better in the short term, such as drinking too much coffee or alcohol, comfort-eating or taking drugs (often on prescription) to help them relax. Long-term, these can lead to other problems of addiction that may cause more stress, starting another stress cycle.

Stress is not all bad and finding the optimal level of stress that can help you perform just a little better is helpful. But chronic stress has a negative impact on your physical health, short-term ability to concentrate, think and reason, and on your emotional intelligence and social interaction.

Stressed Out is Not the New Normal

Stress seems to be accepted as the way we live our lives these days. As we've seen it is not helpful to getting ahead at work, or being healthy in the long term. So, you do need to keep your stress at the optimal level. The next chapter looks at ways you can manage your stress and your energy levels so that you are better able to focus. But first I suggest that you take a few minutes to assess your own stress levels and stress responses using the self-assessment *My Personal Stress Response* in the appendix.

 Tip 8: Assess your physical, psychological and behavioural responses to stress. Be aware of when your stress levels rise and what your typical reactions are and implement some of the tips from the next chapter to lower your stress.

The stress self-assessment looks at many of the common reactions people have when feeling stressed. The aim is to recognise your typical response to stress from how you feel (psychological) or how you act (behavioural) or how your body reacts (physical). From here, then you know what behaviour, thought patterns, psychological and physical reactions are the indicators to tell you that you are feeling stressed. This awareness then allows you to put in place a coping strategy (based on the tips in the next chapter) that help you to manage your stress levels and regain your energy levels.

If you're feeling stressed for a long time, you don't notice your stress response any more. It starts to become the "normal" way you are feeling. You stop noticing strange or odd things in the way you are feeling emotionally or physically or how you are behaving. You start to accept them as the way it is, or think they are a result of some other issue.

Symptoms
of Stress

Psychological

Angry
Anxious
Apprehensive
Frightened, worrying thoughts
Ashamed, embarrassed
Depressed or feeling low
Guilty
Jealous
Mood swings
Reduced self-esteem
Feeling out of control
Unable to concentrate
Negative thoughts and images
Images of being out of control
Increased daydreaming

Physical

Dry mouth
Clammy hands
Frequent colds and infections
Palpitations or racing heartbeat
Breathlessness
Tightness or pain in the chest
Migraines or tension headaches
Vague aches and pains
Backaches
Indigestion
Diarrhoea
Constipation
Irritable bowel syndrome
Skin complaints or allergies
Asthma attacks

Behavioural

Passive behaviour
Aggressive behaviour
Irritability, snappiness
Increased alcohol consumption
Increased caffeine consumption
Comfort eating
Disturbed sleep patterns
Withdrawal or sulking
Clenched fists, banging table, tapping foot or hand
Compulsive or impulsive behaviour e.g. checking rituals
Poor time management
Reduced work performance
Increased absenteeism from work

A friend of mine thought that his heart palpitations would stop if he cut back his coffee intake from six or seven cups a day to one or two cups. Eventually when he cut out all caffeine and the heart palpitations still continued, he went to the doctor convinced he was going to be told he had some serious heart condition. After ECGs and various other (expensive) tests, the doctor told him the heart palpitations were stress-related. Often it is hard to separate out the symptoms that are stress-related from other physical symptoms that are related to other conditions.

We start to believe that it is "normal" to be stressed if you have a busy job. It's seen as coming with the territory, along with the managerial title. There is certainly a lot more pressure in today's business because the pace of business is moving faster, customer expectations are raised and yet we have decreased resources. However, in the end it is not how much pressure there is, but your response to that pressure which determines if it leads to psychological and physical stress. The next chapter has some suggestions how you can manage your response to stress.

Chapter Recap

- *Stress is your response to pressure. Your physical and psychological responses determine how you cope with stress.*

- *Physically our bodies were not designed to manage the stress of a modern world.*

- *Psychologically and behaviourally, we manage stress very differently, depending on our upbringing, personality, belief system and learned behaviours.*

- *Assess your physical, psychological and behavioural responses to stress with the self-assessment in the appendix. Be aware of when your stress levels rise and what your typical reactions and symptoms are.*

- *Use the tips in the next chapter to manage your stress levels to be in the optimal zone.*

CHAPTER 3:

Stress Less

It's not stress that kills us, it is our reaction to it.

- Hans Selye

You've now identified the stress symptoms that frequently come out when you are under pressure. It can be how you feel (psychological) or how you act (behavioural) or how your body reacts (physical). Now that you can recognise that you are feeling stressed, the next step is to change your response to the pressure and lower your stress levels. If you ask around a few people that you know how they manage stress, you will get many different answers, from excessive exercise to relaxing meditation. This is because stress is a mix of our physical reactions, our psychological make-up and behaviours that all play together.

It is important to look at ways to deal with both the physical and psychological side. The physical side is more preventative and helps you deal with the symptoms of stress, so is a way of coping better with the pressure so you don't get so stressed. The psychological side starts to look at the issues that are stressing you and see how you can redefine and deal with the issue.

Exercising Away the Stress Demons

We all know that exercise is good for your body. It helps prevent illnesses like heart disease and strokes and helps to manage our weight. People who exercise live longer. But new research is finding that exercise is also good for the mind, especially in managing stress.

The physical changes that happen under a stressful situation as the body gets prepared for flight or fight means adrenaline and cortisol are flooding the body and brain. These neurochemicals are not helping you to be sharp, focused and creative. When you exercise you reduce the levels of adrenaline and cortisol in your body and brain helping to clear your mind. This allows you to improve your attention and focus.

When you exercise, a second, feel-good chemical is released into the blood system called endorphins. Endorphins are similar to morphine, so help to block pain. This feel-good hit after exercise is sometimes known as the runner's high from the experience of marathon runners. But you can get the same boost with other forms of exercise. Happening at the same time in the brain, the chemical noradrenaline, which is the opposite to adrenaline, is released, helping you to relax and calm down. Serotonin is also released and this helps improve your mood. Too little serotonin is associated with depression.

Exercise also helps you to re-focus. It is hard to worry about a work problem when you're concentrating on where to put your feet when you're jogging on uneven ground, or where to hit the ball when playing tennis or golf. Through exercise, you re-focus, and along with your feel-good hit of endorphins, you reduce stress and improve your concentration.

Some of the most interesting recent research showed that brain capacity increased in a group of adults who exercised in comparison to a group who did no exercise. Using an MRI scan, the researchers found the active group had more connections in the area of the brain responsible for memory, the hippocampus[26].

The good news is that to improve your concentration and focus, you don't need to be a weekend warrior who runs marathons or does the Ironman. Thirty to sixty minutes of walking, three times a week has positive effects on the brain, reducing stress and putting you in a productive brain state[27]. Even as little as ten minutes a day was shown to boost school children's concentration. The group of kids who had exercised for just ten minutes were better able to block out distractions and were more able to focus compared to a group that did no exercise[28].

Exercise often is high on the agenda of things people know they should do, but comes well down on the agenda of things that they actually do. But if you look at exercise being something small and simple, then it is more likely to happen. I went through the stress review (as in the last chapter) with a client, Vera, and she realised that she'd cut out her usual lunch time walk as she'd got busier in her job. She thought she'd be more productive by eating at her desk and pushing on. We set a goal starting with a ten-minute walk over the lunch hour. She found it was worth the time as she was able to re-focus and be more productive in the afternoon with a clear head, and avoided so many crumbs on the keyboard!

A study into the work-life balance of engineers found that regular exercise was one of the key factors in whether the engineers managed their work-life balance effectively. The engineers all worked in the same team, with the same boss, the same workload and job title. The ones who exercised regularly were more able to balance their work and life, in comparison to the other engineers who felt overwhelmed and stressed. Some would exercise when they felt stressed or when tackling a difficult problem and felt they were better able to solve the problem after taking a break for a run.

 Tip 9: Exercise to reduce stress: Even a 10-minute short walk can be enough to refocus and improve your concentration, especially if you can get out in the fresh air.

Snooze You Lose – Or Do You?

Sleep and stress are tightly linked. While scientists are not completely sure what the purpose of sleep is, it is very clear that without it we are more easily stressed and less able to focus and concentrate. Sleep deprivation is a form of torture used by various military forces. One of the first symptoms of even moderate sleep loss is the inability to control your emotions, followed by irrationality and disordered thinking. So, if you want someone to tell you a secret then, as the military knows they are more likely to divulge it when they are tired.

Even a moderate amount of sleep deprivation impairs performance significantly. After 16-17 hours of being awake, (say from 6 am to after midnight, similar to a full day's work followed by hours of web surfing after dinner), cognitive performance is reduced to the same extent as driving drunk (with a limit of 0.05% blood alcohol content) with slowed reaction times, decreased awareness and impaired judgment.

A lack of sleep reduces the performance of our prefrontal cortex, which manages the executive functions, processes information, manages multiple tasks and reviews thoughts. The functions most affected by a lack of sleep are high level functions needed to perform well in a professional position: creativity, decision-making, adaptability and emotional control[29].

Lack of sleep

Lack of sleep people feel they are:

- Less able to focus in meetings (69%)
- Took longer to complete tasks (68%)
- Challenged to generate new ideas (60%)
- More irritable and less able to control their emotions (84%)
- More stressed and less able to think clearly (75%)

Survey of 1000 international professional people by Ashridge Business School

Effects of Lack of Sleep (Ashridge Business School Survey)

All of this leads to low productivity and less effective working. Consider the time it takes to rebuild a relationship after an argument with a colleague, when a few more hours of sleep could have meant you had better emotional control and handled the discussion better.

Many of us could be said to be sleep deprived: 40% of Americans are not getting enough sleep[30], 40% of people in the UK are getting less than 6 hours' sleep[31] and 35% of Australians say they wake up feeling unrefreshed[32]. People are torturing themselves through their own choice of working longer and sleeping less. Arianna Huffington in her book *The Sleep Revolution* describes the irony that people will forgo sleep in the name of productivity, but productivity is substantially reduced when we are sleep deprived. The book was written about the importance of sleep after Arianna Huffington physically crashed with complete exhaustion. In a very dramatic style, she describes a life of sleeping 3-4 hours a night and believing she was thriving on it. One evening she woke up at her desk with blood all around her, and no idea how she got there. She was so tired and exhausted, she had fallen asleep and hit her head.

My story is less dramatic than Arianna's. I worked in an organisation where long hours were valued and I got sucked into working long hours, without consciously questioning it. One of my bosses would frequently pull an "all-nighter". Rather than this being considered a bad habit, it was seen as evidence of the hard work required to get to the top. I also got into the habit of working long hours. But the following day when looking at work done at 2 am in the morning, I would see it was riddled with errors. Generally, I was achieving less even though I'd worked harder. After a couple of all-nighters with limited sleep, I'd be very snappy and irritable.

Several years later after both I and that boss had left the company and moved on to new jobs, we heard how a new CEO had taken over. Many of the projects we'd worked so hard on late into the night, were now disestablished. We joked, half seriously, we should remember this when working late in our new jobs.

Technology means we can be on the go, 24/7. Right up until the minute that we go to sleep we can be checking our smartphones, and if we sleep with our smartphone next to the bed (as 70% of Americans do[33]) we check them again from the minute that we wake up. The blue light from the small screen on a mobile device is like daylight. It fools the body into thinking that it is time to be awake, increasing alertness[34]. But it's not just the light that impacts on our sleep, it is the content of what we are doing. After playing a video game or answering emails, it's harder to fall asleep than after reading an e-book. It's not easy to get to sleep just after you have been reading an email about a work issue. It takes time for the body and brain to wind down into a good sleep pattern.

Think about how we deal with our children: we create a ritual to calm them down after a busy day to get them to off to bed and sleep. Perhaps starting with bath time, reading a bedtime story while snuggled in bed, some gentle sounds from a music box and then finally lights out. But as adults, we work up to the minute we go to bed and wonder why we don't go straight to sleep. We too need to create our own ritual so we are relaxed and ready to sleep.

Tip 10: Use 5-4-3-2-1 tip to create a sleep ritual so that you are ready to go to sleep.

5: Five hours before going to sleep, try to avoid caffeinated drinks.

4: Four hours before going to sleep, try to avoid drinking alcohol. Alcohol might help you get to sleep initially but disrupts the cycle for staying asleep, meaning you sleep lighter and wake up more often.

3: Three hours before going to sleep, try to avoid eating a heavy meal. Like alcohol, it might make you sleepy, but is then likely to disrupt your sleep pattern later in the night.

2: Two hours before going to sleep, try to stop working. Have time to switch off your thoughts from work.

1: One hour before going to sleep, try not to be using any small screen devices that emit blue light. Try reading a paper-based device instead, i.e. a book or magazine!

For some, getting to sleep isn't the problem but staying asleep is the challenge. Here meditation, which is covered in the next section, is useful to try at times when you are tossing and turning in the early hours. But if you haven't already learned some meditation techniques, then trying to start at 2 am is not the best idea. A quick fix after about 30 minutes of lying awake is to get up and write down all the things that are on your mind. Then try going back to bed and see if this helps you go to sleep.

SLEEP RITUAL

FIVE HOURS
before going to sleep

Try to avoid caffeinated drinks.

FOUR HOURS
before going to sleep

Try to avoid drinking alcohol. Alcohol might help you get to sleep but disrupts the sleep cycle to stay asleep, meaning you sleep lighter and wake up more often.

THREE HOURS
before going to sleep

Try to avoid eating a heavy meal. Like alcohol it might make you sleepy but is then likely to disrupt your sleep pattern later in the night.

TWO HOURS
before going to sleep

Try to stop working to have time to switch off your thoughts from work.

ONE HOUR
before going to sleep

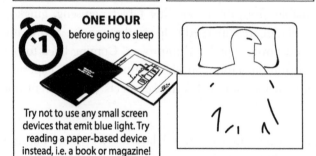

Try not to use any small screen devices that emit blue light. Try reading a paper-based device instead, i.e. a book or magazine!

Sleep Ritual

Sleep is a highly individual experience. A normal person requires seven hours, but who is "normal"? Like most things in life, there will always be people who make it into the Guinness Book of Records[35] or an Olympics sports team, who, due to their unique combination of physical features and psychological traits, can live with less sleep. The question is – are you that one-in-a-million person? There are some people who can function normally with three to four hours' sleep, but if you are not one of them, then to improve your productivity, sleep more and don't work long into the night.

Eat, Drink and Be Merry, Not Weary

Every week it seems there is a new headline telling you some latest fact (or fiction) about food, diets, superfoods, vitamins, herbs, smoothies and fasting cures. One week we read a headline telling us that red wine and dark chocolate are good for you. Just as you stop feeling guilty about your glass of wine and bar of chocolate, along comes another headline telling us the opposite. And when it comes to concentration and focus, there is no shortage of advice and supplements available, from brain boosting tablets, ginseng, gingko to fish oil. All are supposed help you be smarter. Sadly, much is rather over-hyped and unproven. Coming back to plain old common sense, you know from your own experience that your food and drink intake affects your concentration and focus.

If you've not eaten for several days (had a stomach bug, gone on a highly restrictive diet or fasted) you'll know that after 24-48 hours you will start feel lightheaded and certainly you will not be functioning at your peak of alertness. Being hungry, it is hard to concentrate. Being dehydrated and hungry, then concentration can be impossible. But it seems even a skipped meal can have a negative impact on your concentration. "Breakfast in Schools" is a programme run in the USA (in 2012) to give 13 million kids a nutritious breakfast as educationalists found that children perform much better academically, behave better and are healthier after eating a nutritious breakfast.

Basically, our brain needs calories to function well and skipping breakfast means it is deprived of calories all night until midday. Too often during the working day, we are rushing between meetings, skipping meals, grabbing a snack from the vending machine or just any convenience food so we get something to eat. Working in a global company, it is hard to hold a teleconference that is not going to be crossing someone's lunch time, breakfast or dinner time.

On the other side, too much food or too many calories make you less able to concentrate. You know that heavy-headed, droopy eyelid feeling after the Sunday roast at grandma's house, especially if it is hot and stuffy. Or when you're sitting at your desk (or worse, in a meeting) after a lunch of cheesy pasta!

Most of us know that coffee and sugar will give us a concentration boost as a temporary fix. Depending on the strength of your coffee and your tolerance for caffeine, it will give you a pick-me-up that lasts about 20-30 minutes[36]. Too much sugar generally results in an initial boost followed within about an hour by a sugar crash and a dip in concentration[37]. Your concentration and focus dip to a level below that prior to the coffee and sugar. You can keep drinking more coffee or Coke or energy drinks, keep eating more sugary food but the side effect will eventually be extra pounds on your waistline and an addiction to caffeine.

You don't need to live on rabbit food, but junk food, (high in sugar and fats and empty calories), while it may give you an instant concentration boost, it won't last. It might feel that the 10-15 minutes you need to go and get something healthy for lunch, or to make something to bring to work, is time you just don't have. But in the end, the healthy lunch will have a more positive impact on your ability to concentrate for the afternoon. You'll find you are more productive and you will make up the time it took to get it or prepare it.

Have you seen this before? Put too many people in a small, hot meeting room and remove all water or other fluids. Watch closely and you can soon see the effects of dehydration. People will become drowsy, find it hard to concentrate and get irritable. Add a boring speaker and you will be able to feel the energy drain out of the room faster than the speed of light. Result: there will be no great thinking and problem-solving going on in that meeting.

Researchers compared people's performance and mood when they were mildly dehydrated and when not. They found that even mild dehydration made it harder to concentrate, impaired short-term memory and caused mood swings. Mild dehydration means we don't even notice we are thirsty enough to have a drink.[38]

There is a saying that with healthy living, you don't actually live longer, it just feels like it. While this is rather cynical (as the evidence does show on average that with a healthy lifestyle, people do live longer), the point is made that it is all about moderation. It is not about a special diet, supplements, vitamins, superfoods or energy drinks. A sensible regular diet, avoiding too much caffeine and sugar, together with sufficient water to keep you hydrated, will help you maintain your concentration throughout the day.

Tip 11: Keep hydrated, avoid heavy food, excessive sugar and caffeine to help you concentrate.

Psychological Health

For our focus and attention to be at their peak, managing our mind is just as important as managing our physical body. It is a skill, which, like many others, takes time and self-awareness to learn. If you're stressed, you will be feeling busy, overwhelmed and overloaded from all different angles, you will be making mistakes, becoming forgetful, finding it hard to control your emotions and not making good decisions. Finding a way to escape the stress for even a very short period of calm inside your mind in an otherwise crazy world can really help. This gives you a chance to reset and re-focus then go back to your work priorities. Here are several ways you can reset, re-focus and reduce your stress levels.

Hit the Reset Switch with Meditation

Meditation might invoke some images of a scene from the film and book *Eat, Pray, Love* where Elizabeth Gilbert escaped her busy life to live for six months at an ashram in India and learned how to meditate (and wrote a bestselling novel about the experience). While meditation requires some training, it doesn't mean you must completely throw away your current life and move to another continent. With some practice, you can learn short meditation techniques of about 10 minutes to bring back some calm to your otherwise hectic day.

Our minds wander about half the time (or 46.9% of the time to be exact) according to research at Harvard Medical School[39] . But to gain the benefits of meditation to improve your attention doesn't need to be an intense experience, and doesn't even require you to sit cross-legged on the floor and burn incense. People who have undergone meditation training over a period of one to three months are more able to concentrate and are less prone to mind-wandering[40]. Even short periods of meditation can have an impact on your attention span, as has been proven with complete novices practising for 20 minutes over five days, able to improve their concentration[41]. A short meditation pause during working hours can help improve attention and help you regain a more productive mindset.

While I am sure that some of the monks in Tibet are going to be appalled at this suggestion, I have recommended to several of my clients to learn meditation via an app and tried it myself. It is a simple and practical way to learn how to calm your mind and re-focus, even if it just means taking a few minutes during a busy work day. A couple of apps I often recommend to clients can be found in the appendix.

One of my clients described meditation as doing her "mental fitness training". She was highly energised and focused on restarting her business in a new country after having relocated because of her husband's job. However, re-establishing your business in a new country takes some time and she was getting very frustrated at how long it was taking. She started using the Headspace app at the start of the day, just for 10 minutes, and she felt calmer and in control, more accepting of the frustrations. By being less impatient and agitated, she felt she could achieve more.

Mindfulness

Mindfulness feels like a bit of fad. If you Google *mindfulness,* you get 44 million hits, 37.5 million more than if you

Googled it 10 years ago. There are 8,000 books available on Amazon and there is everything from mindfulness apps to mindfulness colouring-in books available. But like most fads, there is a part which is valuable, and a part which is over-hyped. The core of mindfulness is very useful in calming and concentrating your mind so you can focus on what needs to be done.

Our view of the world is perceived through our own unique lens. Whenever we see something, hear something or sense something, we start analysing what it means, what it reminds us of in the past, and where it is going in the future. We are constantly judging, categorising and analysing. Then we react to these thoughts (whether we are aware of our reaction or not), giving rise to emotions. Mindfulness is about stopping judging, analysing and planning, even for a short period of time. It is about being present in the here and now, not dwelling on what happened in the past or planning the future. At the same time, mindfulness is about being aware of your thoughts and emotions without judging them.

Mindfulness roots go back east to Buddhist traditions, but modern mindfulness blends in theory from western psychology. What is the most compelling is that there is strong evidence from over 35 different studies showing that mindfulness reduces people's levels of stress, improves their wellbeing, mood and vitality,[42] and improves attention and focus[43].

Mindfulness is best taught within a course but an app, book or video can also work. One of the most well-known courses in Mindfulness-Based Stress Reduction (MBSR) is a short programme developed by Jon Kabat-Zinn from the University of Massachusetts Medical School. These programmes combine key elements of mindfulness from east and west. Different forms of eastern meditation and yoga practices are blended with more analytical practices from western psychology, such as identifying stressors and reframing. This MBSR course has been around for 35 years and found to be effective in reducing stress and improving wellbeing[44].

I attended an MBSR course over an eight-week period and the main take-away for me was that it made me rethink my ultra-busy lifestyle. I tended to think that doing more was better in all parts of my life, not just in my career. Weekends would be full of activities from skiing to cycling to hiking to running. And there was usually a goal there, to be faster than the last time I'd run this route or to get to the top in under two hours. The main realisation that came to me is that there needed to be some time to wind down. My weekend activities should be relaxing and enjoyable, not training hard to break the record of fastest time. Pushing myself too hard mentally for five days a week and physically for two days of the week was also leading to a lot of physical aches and pains, along with mental exhaustion.

I still keep in touch with some of the people I met on the MBSR programme, now three years ago. Interestingly, many of them have gone on to make changes in their jobs or lives. Some of these are quite small changes. There's Alex, who worked in a high-pressured hedge fund trading job where he often felt very angry at his boss. He learned to put some distance between himself and his emotions and manage the situation better. Kate decided that her job as a director in a large corporate bank was not where she wanted to spend the next 20 years of her career. She is now setting up her own tourism company.

Tip 12: Try mindfulness or meditation to manage your stress levels, and improve your attention and focus.

From Music, Massage and Yoga to Rock Climbing

There are, of course, many other ways that people find to relax and switch off. And if it isn't a mind-altering addictive substance and if it works, then just do it. Meditation and mindfulness are two techniques that have evidence to show they work to improve attention. There are lots of techniques that help people relax their mind and body. Having a dedicated period of time to relax then increases your focus when you return to your work. Spending time relaxing, doing yoga or meditation might feel as if you are doing nothing, but in the end, it helps you to be more productive. A few other ways to relax that are worth a brief mention are music, massage, or a hobby that requires intense concentration.

The debate about the benefits of music on your concentration has raged in most families with teenagers for decades. Generally, teenagers like to study with music on, while their parents believe that study is better in silence. To their dismay, there is no clear winner for this debate in the research. It seems the best answer that can be given is it depends on the type of work that is being done. For repetitive work in a factory, background music has been shown to help productivity[45]. For school children, pleasant music improved performance on more routine tasks. However, for complex problems, any music reduced performance[46].

There is more evidence that certain music can reduce stress, or lessen the impact of stress. The music that people typically find relaxing is instrumental, classical or electronic, with about 60 beats per minute. On the other hand, some people find such music grating and doesn't help their concentration at all.

While the scientists debate and continue their research, pragmatically many people know music helps to change your mood. Think of a few phrases of an upbeat song you know and hum them to yourself and see if it changes your mood. If you can't think of a song then hum the words *"…I gotta feeling that tonight's gonna be a good, good night, That tonight's gonna be a good, good night…"*[47] and see if you feel more energised. On the other hand, you will find Enya's *Waterfall* very relaxing[48]. Save some mood-altering songs into your playlist and listen to it when you need to relax and re-focus. Another advantage to listening to music in the office through your headphones is that you'll probably get asked fewer questions than if you were sitting at your desk with your eyes closed, meditating.

Some people swear by the benefits of yoga, tai chi and similar activities that have an element that focus mindfulness together with repetitive movements. Improving your attention and focus is achieved with the relaxation and meditative aspects. There are other more vigorous activities that require a similar focus of physical movement and mental concentration like rock climbing or dancing.

Massage also relaxes physically with the aid of soothing music, warm lighting and a feeling of looking after yourself; it helps you to mentally relax too. An acquaintance of mine who not only has a highly stressful job dealing with ultra-high net worth clients for one of the big banks, but two small children as well, swears by her weekly massages to help her relax and re-energise.

1. Marconi Union - Weightless
2. Airstream - Electra
3. Enya – Watermark
4. Coldplay – Strawberry Swing
5. Barcelona – Please Don't Go
6. Adele – Someone Like You
7. Mogawi –Take me Somewhere Nice
8. Dido – Thank you
9. Norah Jones- I don't know Why
10. Fink – Looking too Closely

♪ Relaxing music

Playlist of Relaxing Music

A hobby that requires intense concentration like playing a musical instrument, painting, drawing or even doing crosswords or sudoku can also help you to feel re-focused and relaxed. The intense concentration may not seem as if you are relaxing, but once you've reached a point where you have mastered the skill, shifting your focus away from your work helps refresh the brain.

What might feel like unproductive time listening to music, meditating or doing a crossword, will actually help you be more productive when you return to your work. When you get busy, then it is easy to think of cutting out these "nice to haves" or "time wasters" like a massage or a crossword puzzle. But to be more efficient, it requires taking this time to relax and switch gears, so you regain the mental energy to be more efficient and productive again.

 Tip 13: If it relaxes you, and it is not an illicit substance or illegal, then don't drop it when you get busy. The relaxation will help improve your concentration and focus.

Stressed About Stress

The same situation can make one person feel very stressed, whereas another person can feel completely at ease or even excited. Researchers have been trying to understand this puzzle for years, looking at personality, self-confidence, upbringing, experiences, how we've coped with stress in the past and other stressors we could be experiencing in life. There is some validity to all of these variables, but one of the most interesting individual differences to emerge in recent years is how you **think** about stress. In short if you think that something is going to be stressful, and you regard stress as bad, then it is a self-fulfilling prophecy, you **will** be stressed out.

The word stress is considered by most people to be something negative. As we saw in the earlier section in Chapter 2 when we looked at the inverted U diagram, a certain amount of stress is useful to help you perform better, like for an exam or for an important presentation. Too much stress will affect your performance negatively. For example, the right amount of stress makes you focus and work hard during an exam, whereas too much stress and your mind goes blank ("brain freeze"). Likewise, some stress will help you to prepare well for a presentation, but too much will make you sweat and shake in front of the audience.

So, one of the things that you can do is try to reframe your thinking around a stressful event. This is quite a simple technique but also very challenging. Imagine having a conversation with your friend where you are trying to help them, gently, to look at a problem in a different way. Instead, you're having the conversation with yourself. So first you need to understand what you are thinking, and then it's like reprogramming your thoughts about the issue.

Let's start with the case, surprisingly familiar, of James who doesn't like giving presentations to large audiences. James is a partner at a large tax consultancy firm and once a year he must give a presentation to the whole company. Because he doesn't like the annual presentation, his stress builds up and causes his hands to shake and his mouth gets dry. When these reactions start, he thinks everyone is noticing and he gets more stressed and starts to sweat, worried that he looks bad.

What the reframing technique aims to do is to think about giving the presentation in a way that doesn't induce further stress. It is known as changing the thoughts from Stress Induced Thinking (SITs) to Stress Alleviating Thinking (SATs)

Here's how it would look in James' case:

SIT: I'm terrible at giving presentations, it is going to be just dreadful.

SAT: *Giving presentations may not be my best skill, but I have done it before at the last few years' annual conferences, and I didn't do so badly.*

SIT: Everyone will notice that my hands are shaking and know that I am nervous.

SAT: *If my hands are shaking I can put them on the podium and people won't notice it at all. If people see that I am nervous then that is not so bad – they know I am a good tax consultant and don't usually speak at large events.*

SIT: My mouth will go dry and I won't be able to speak.

SAT: *I have water there, if my mouth goes dry then I can take a sip of water.*

SIT: I might start sweating and it looks terrible.

SAT: *I will make sure I have a tissue and can wipe my face if I feel sweaty.*

This is not some positive thinking mantra where you repeat "I am great" or similar. This is about trying to understand the thoughts that are making you feel stressed and then break the vicious cycle of thoughts that are making you more stressed. You need to be able to recognise what you are thinking to yourself that could cause you additional stress. In this case "I am terrible at this", or "it will be dreadful" are common thoughts people might have. Worst-case scenarios come to mind with very dramatic language.

In a coaching session, I might ask, "What is the worst thing that could happen if people found out you are not good at public speaking?" When people answer out loud, they suddenly realise that they sound ridiculous saying "people won't respect me". By toning down the disaster-thinking or taking away the worst-case scenario and replacing it with a more reasonable thought, then their stress is reduced. In this case with lowered stress then the likely physical reactions like sweating, dry mouth and shaking hands are also likely to be toned down.

Kelly McGonigal's TED talk on making stress your friend is one of the most popular talks on YouTube with 13 million views[49]. Based on the research she quotes in this talk, reframing how you think about stress could have a huge impact on managing stress. If you think that something is going to be stressful and you are worried about this stress then it will just stress you more. Over the long term, this impacts on your health. However, if you see the stress response in your body as helping you prepare for the situation and helping you perform better, then it has no negative impact on your health.

 Tip 14: Turn your Stress Induced Thinking (SIT's) into Stress Alleviating Thinking (SAT's) to reframe your mindset about stress.

Stress Less and Focus More

Being focused, attentive and productive is easier to do if your stress is at an optimal level. Just enough stress to excite you to perform well, not too much stress to push you over the edge. Pressure leads to reactions in our body and brain that are not suited for the modern world. These reactions were highly adaptive reactions millions of years ago in a very different world. So, if you want to think straight, then being at the optimal level of stress is important. As we are all different, the strategies that are effective in helping us deal with stress will be very different too. Try a few of these tips and find the one that works best for you.

Chapter Recap

- *Use the 5-4-3-2-1 tip to create a sleep ritual so that you are ready to go to sleep:*

  5: Five hours before going to sleep, try to avoid caffeinated drinks.

  4: Four hours before going to sleep try to avoid drinking alcohol. Alcohol might help you get to sleep but disrupts the cycle for staying asleep, meaning you sleep lighter and wake up more often.

  3: Three hours before going to sleep, try to avoid eating a heavy meal; just as alcohol might make you sleepy, it is then likely to disrupt your sleep pattern later in the night.

  2: Try to stop working two hours before going to sleep to have time to switch off your thoughts from work.

  1: One hour before going to sleep, try not to be using any small screen devices that emit blue light. Try reading a paper-based device instead, i.e. a book or magazine!

- *Keep hydrated, avoid heavy food, excessive sugar and caffeine to help you concentrate.*

- *Try mindfulness or meditation to manage your stress levels, and improve your attention and focus.*

- *If it relaxes you, and it is not an illicit substance or illegal, then don't drop it when you get busy. The relaxation will help improve your concentration and focus. In the end, you will be more productive.*

- *Turn your Stress Induced Thinking (SITs) into Stress Alleviating Thinking (SATs) to reframe your mindset about stress.*

CHAPTER 4:

Get the Right Mindset and Get More Done

Working hard for something we don't care about is called stress: Working hard for something we love is called passion.

- Simon Sinek

There are those times when it feels like it has come together perfectly. You're sharp, you're focused, you're so into the topic that it's easy. If you are preparing a presentation, it is crystal clear what you want to say, or if you are working on a complex problem, suddenly it seems the answer is so obvious. These moments are called "flow". These moments of flow seem to be less frequent in business, more frequent when you are doing your favourite hobby or sport. In the last two chapters, we looked at how to avoid stress so you can think straight. In this chapter we now take it up a level to how to get into a highly productive, focused and concentrated mode of working.

Living for the Weekend

Why is it easy to get excited about the weekends? Because you get the opportunity to do the things that you want to do. At work, we are often doing something that someone else wants us to do. It may not be that your boss gives you direct orders, but it could well be that you're working on a project or task that you are just not that excited about. For me when I worked in Human Resources roles, there were two sides of the job. The enjoyable part was where you are out there dealing with people like recruiting, training, facilitating, and working on projects that help engage people in the organisation. The other part is work I didn't like as much, less to do with people and more to do with administration like collating data or sorting out issues with the HR information system. It was easy to motivate myself about the part of my job I liked, but much harder for the part I didn't like. Somehow the tasks I liked less would always be left till the last minute, until finally forced to do it just before the deadline. Then they were often done badly so there were more mistakes than there should have been.

We are usually more motivated at weekends because it is our own goal. So how can we motivate ourselves to do a work task we don't like? It needs to become a goal we **want** to do, not one we **must** do. To do this, it is important to understand why we are motivated by some things and not others. When we understand our motivations and drivers then we can understand how we can help to motivate ourselves to do things that we are not that excited about. Put quite simply, in my case I like to deal with people, but not data. In this case, my trick was to imagine the person behind it. So, if I had to prepare a contract for a new employee that I'd spent time talking to and had got to know, then it was not a problem to concentrate to get it right for them. But to prepare a headcount report for a meeting I never attended, I had low motivation as there was no people interest.

Understanding the impact your job has on others or the bigger picture motivates us. An experiment by psychologist Adam Grant[50] involved a group of students doing a very mundane job where they had to call people and ask for donations to a university. A lot of the time they got rejections, and as it was just a way for the students to earn some money, there was no long-term career path. In the experiment, one group heard a short talk from a student who had received a scholarship as a result of the donations and the impact it had had on his life. The other group didn't. Over the next few weeks they found those who had heard from the student who received the scholarship were much more motivated and collected twice as many donations as the group that hadn't.

The lesson for us to get motivated is to understand not just why we are doing something, but also to see a purpose or the bigger picture and how it benefits others. If the purpose is aligned to our personal values, then it works even better. You can also use this if you have to give someone a relatively mundane task to do. Explain to them the significance of what they are doing, for example how it helps the business or to improve something for somebody. Then set clear expectations and you will likely find that their motivation levels will be much higher.

If you think that something is pointless then it is hard to get motivated. Another social science experiment[51] looked at how pointless work is demotivating. A group of students were recruited to build Lego models and were paid $2.00

for assembling the first one. After assembling it, those conducting the experiment told the person they could build another model, but this time they would be paid $1.89 and were asked if they wanted to stop. For one group, the experimenters placed the first completed model to the side of the table. With the other group, the experimenter started disassembling the model as the person was working on the next one. The price for building a third, fourth, and fifth Lego model kept dropping. Each time they were asked if they wanted to stop. For the group where the Lego model was disassembled in front of them, they pulled out at $1.40. The other group, where their model was just put to the side, kept working until the payment was $1.01. So, if you think what you are doing is pointless or a waste of time then it is hard to get much motivation to do it, even if you are getting paid for it.

Unfortunately, there are those things that you have to do that even if you do understand the purpose behind it, it still doesn't motivate you. For me it was collecting data to show cost savings after a restructuring project. I disliked the restructuring project and disliked even more having to reduce all the people who had been made redundant to dollars and cents. There was little way to motivate myself for any higher purpose as it went against my values. I used to reward myself to do it, just like you'd motivate your pet dog, "If you're a good boy Rover, then you can have a doggy treat". So I'd tell myself that if I did this report, then I would allow myself a coffee break while surfing the internet for my next holiday.

This sort of instant reward can work for an unenjoyable task that takes a couple of hours a month, while the rest of the job is enjoyable. If that task was the main focus of the job, I know I wouldn't be very happy in my work. Then the question would arise if I should move on to a different job, or even change career.

 Tip 15: Make your work goals your own goals. Understand the purpose or reason you are working towards this goal. If you can't do that, then reward yourself for having completed a step.

Feel the Buzz of Progress

Making progress towards your goals can give you a real sense of achievement and make you want to do more. But when seeing progress can be unclear is when the goal is too big or too far away, and especially if the goal is vague. In a company where there is reasonable leadership, then there is usually a clear goal, and in some cases, a clear project plan and a clear line of sight to the target. Often though, it is not so clear and we struggle to achieve goals that seem to be too big and vague.

One of my coaching clients, Sarah, wanted to set up her own business. Sarah really wanted to do it, so she should have been highly motivated. Sarah came to me for coaching as she was feeling disappointed and frustrated as she felt she was not making any progress. One of the key things that we found helped her was to break down the huge goal of starting a business into some smaller goals so they seemed achievable. For example, we broke it down into a list of marketing the business, finding an office etc. She then went away and worked on sub-tasks under these and set some timeframes, just like a project plan. It made it much easier for her to see progress towards the bigger goal and start to realise her dream of having her own business.

We get a real buzz when we make some progress towards our goals. In a huge study of over 200 professionals across many industries, Therese Amabile[52] reviewed journals written by people about their daily work. She looked in the journals for the things that made people happiest at work. The biggest buzz people got out of work was when they were making progress towards something, they'd solved a problem, they achieved a step along the way. Set yourself some small steps towards your big goal, check off when you've reached them and you'll feel a buzz of achievement. This feeling of achievement will help keep you motivated towards the bigger goal.

 Tip 16: Break a big goal down into small steps and feel the buzz of progress when achieving these steps.

The Glass is Empty

Viewing the glass half full or half empty is supposed to tell us if a person is an optimist or a pessimist. But if you're in a really bad mood then it is like the glass has just been spilled all over your new laptop. We've all had days where it feels like one thing after another has gone wrong. It usually starts with one small thing going wrong first thing in the morning, like the coffee machine breaking down while making your morning coffee, that sets you up to see everything else in the day going wrong. But is it really that so many bad things have happened in your day, or just that you are looking through your "bad day" lens, so you start noticing and counting them? If you set up that intention and put your brain into a defensive mode scanning for any problems, you will find small mistakes and make them bigger. We interpret events with the lens or with the mindset that we have.

Half empty

or half full?

Glass Half Full or Half Empty?

Let's take a work example. If you go into a meeting with your boss with the expectation that it will be bad, then the meeting will probably go badly. Imagine you are saying to yourself before the meeting, "My boss makes me so angry, she is always criticising everything I do," then you will probably find you will get upset because you will be interpreting something she says like, "Why did you schedule the go-live date for March?" you will see it as criticism and react defensively. Instead, go into the meeting thinking, "My boss can be quite critical, not just with me but everyone, but she is trying to improve things for the good of the company". Then when she asks that same question, you can see her asking for more information to help her understand the issue.

In the first thought pattern, you are playing your script about the "mean boss" in your head and it causes you to react to her question negatively. But in the second thought pattern, you have more of a chance of coming up with constructive solutions, working cooperatively with your boss and focusing on the work. This is called reframing your thinking. You look at what you are thinking, identify the lens you are viewing the world through and maybe thoughts you weren't aware of surface. Then you reconsider if these thoughts are helpful to achieving your goal, i.e. seeing your boss through the mean boss lens is not helping you work well together. You then decide how to reframe these thoughts into a more balanced view, such as a "tough boss but driving hard for the good of the company".

Reframing is not a positive affirmation you repeat in your mind and hope that all will be ok, but reviewing and changing your mindset about an issue. Without being caught up in negative emotions, you can focus and concentrate on the real issues. You waste time and energy on negative issues. A positive approach helps you perform better.

Employees with a positive attitude were rated as higher performing by their managers, were better at selling, were more creative and solved problems more effectively[53]. They were more sociable so it improved their ability to get along in a team. There were fewer negative consequences: they were less likely to burnout, quit their job, be off sick or get into conflict with others. And for a group of Japanese engineers it even meant they left the office an hour earlier than their less happy colleagues, almost unheard of in Japan where people work very long hours[54].

Tip 17: Reframe your negative mindset. With a positive mindset, you'll be better able to focus and concentrate on getting things done.

Hey Babe, Get Into the Flow State

It sounds like a 1970s drug, this magic state of flow. "Flow" means being so deeply immersed in your work and absorbed with the activity that you forget about time. Time flies as you are so deeply engaged and engrossed. You are intensely focused and concentrated and start achieving your best performance. Sportspeople might describe this as "being in the zone".

"Flow" is a concept first looked at by a Hungarian psychologist with the most unpronounceable name, Mihaly Csikszentmihalyi, in the 1970s, who was fascinated by artists who got completely absorbed in their painting, forgetting sometimes to eat and sleep. He continued to study people in a state of flow for two more decades and came up with his ideas about how and when people get into the state of flow.

Mihaly believed that flow is some sort of state that will occur when three conditions are right:

Flow State

1. There must be the right balance between the challenge of the activity and your skill levels. The activity must be challenging enough to be interesting and pushing your skills, but not so challenging that you are getting frustrated that your skills are not able to achieve what you want.

2. You are very clear about your motivation and why you want to do this activity, because you enjoy it and it gives you pleasure.

3. You get feedback as to how you are performing immediately. If you are painting you are seeing the picture come alive, if you are dancing your steps are fbwing, if you are surfing you have caught the perfect wave.

I also think that in the work context there is a fourth requirement, having time. At work our time is broken into short one-hour blocks between meetings or events. In such a short period of time, it is hard to get into any feeling of flow. For any chance of flow to happen in a work context then you also need to schedule a period of a good two to three hours to work on your most interesting projects.

You could be forgiven for thinking that the flow at work situation got lost in the 20th century, along with flower power, hippies and The Beatles. I can already hear some of the cynics out there asking if you can really achieve flow in a work context. And true, most of the examples cited by researchers and by people describing their flow experience are about sport, artistic pursuits or hobbies. Since most of us are not professional sportspeople or artists, the question is a valid one – is it possible to reach a state of flow in a middle management job in a large corporation?

Mihaly continued to study flow over the next two or more decades and reported people did experience flow at work. Creative professionals like film animators at Pixar studios and designers at Apple are reported to have felt in a state of flow. A surgeon who is deeply concentrating on an operation, a teacher who has a brilliant session where the students really got it, or a scientist who solves a complex problem are all examples of flow. If you've got a really interesting project at work, something you personally are excited about, that you enjoy doing and is challenging you, then you could achieve a state of flow.

Perhaps a state of flow is a very high standard to expect in a daily work routine, compared to a hobby or sport. But there is more chance of it happening if your values, drives and skills are aligned with the job you are doing. For example, if you are a nurse, teacher or social worker and you really don't like dealing with people, then you have very little chance of finding much flow in your work. If you are in a profession that uses your natural strengths and builds on your skills and experience, then there is more chance that you could achieve a flow state. Finding this alignment is important in enjoying your work.

So even if you think achieving flow is impossible, maybe it's time to consider what job would have more chance of bringing you a sense of intrinsic motivation because it is aligned to your values and your personal sense of purpose and strengths.

 Tip 18: Try to find work that flows. Work or projects that align to your personal sense of purpose and strengths, is challenging and you get reward and feedback from it so it will be easier to concentrate and focus on.

Get into the mood, get into the groove and find the right mindset. From a bad mood to the bliss of a flow state, the way we think about our work has a huge impact on whether we can concentrate and focus on our work. If your mind is looking for every excuse not to enjoy work, then it is easy to be distracted. But if you find your purpose of why you want to do the task, gain a sense of achievement from working towards a goal, and feel some sense of purpose in what you are doing, then you will be much better able to focus, concentrate deeply and achieve more.

Chapter Recap

- *Make your work goals your own goals. Understand the purpose or reason you are working towards this goal. If you can't do that then reward yourself for having completed a step.*

- *Break a big goal down into small steps and feel the buzz of progress when achieving these steps.*

- *Reframe your negative mindset. With a positive mindset, you'll be better able to focus and concentrate on getting things done.*

- *Try to find work that flows. Work or projects that align to your personal sense of purpose and strengths, is challenging and you get reward and feedback from it so it will be easier to concentrate and focus on.*

CHAPTER 5:

Build a Wall Around Your Castle

I have never met a woman, or man, who
stated emphatically, "Yes, I have it all."
Because no matter what any of us has – and
how grateful we are for what we have – no
one has it all.

- Sheryl Sandberg

Your home is your castle – or is it? Your home used to be the place where you spent time with your family and for yourself, an oasis away from the hustle and hassle of work. But now with flexible working arrangements and mobile devices, your home can become an extension of your office.

No one would argue that flexible working isn't a good idea. The opportunity to leave work and pick up the kids from school, get through dinner, bath time and bed routines and then log on for a few more hours in the early evening is great for many families. Or being able to join a conference call in your pyjamas without the inconvenience of going into the office at a ridiculously early hour. The advantages of flexible working outweigh the disadvantages, if you control the boundaries between work and life in a way that suits you. If you are not in control of the boundaries between your work and home life, then it has a negative impact on your stress levels and wellbeing.

Home Invasion by Your Smartphone

Let's take a trip back in time, step into the Tardis and go back 20 years. A world before mobile phones, tablets and wifi was in every home and café. What happened when we left the office? Most of the time we stopped working. Of course, we might take a laptop home, or a pile of papers. Perhaps you had a mobile phone but it was basic, mostly used for voice calls and perhaps a text message or two but certainly not with email and access to the internet. You could do some work on your laptop at home over the weekend, but generally didn't send many email messages as it required a complicated, and often slow, connection.

As technology has advanced in leaps and bounds, then clear boundaries between work and home have also leapt and bounded away. You can be at home, on the commute, in a café, in a park, visiting family and friends and you are always able to connect to your email and the internet. Now it is hard to find places where you aren't able to connect. In theory, you can be available for work 24/7, always on, always invading our personal and family time and our private space.

The 24/7 availability has slowly crept in over time, so slowly that perhaps we don't even notice it. Once upon a time, a long, long time ago, we physically left the office and psychologically disconnected too. There was nothing more that could be done until the following morning, or on Monday after the weekend. "Out of sight and out of mind" meant there was a mental break from work.

The changes in technology have probably brought changes in your behaviour that you haven't even noticed. How often do you check your email just before going to bed? And then check it again as soon as you wake up in the morning? Almost a third of people surveyed in the UK say they check their phones within five minutes of waking up and 27% check their phones five minutes before going to sleep[55]. And if you think that is bad, one in ten people admit to having sent a text while having sex[56]. Smartphone addiction has even been given a name, "nomophobia", the fear of being without your phone. If you are worried that you are becoming addicted to your smartphone, you can check by taking the short quiz in the appendix at the back of the book.

Change that creeps up on us is the hardest to recognise, just like the frog in a saucepan of water that is only slowly warming up. Looking back, we see how things have changed. Otherwise we don't notice that we are now constantly tethered to our phones, because it is just the way that everyone is these days. Your home is no longer your castle, your space, your time away from work, but an extension of your office. But it doesn't have to be if you start to build some physical or psychological walls.

Setting Boundaries

Boundaries can be thought of as the demarcation between your work and personal life. Different people have different ways of managing their boundaries. Some people integrate their work and life, some keep it very separate, and others cycle between periods that are work-focused and those that are life-focused. Here's a run-down on the different styles identified in research by Kossek:[57]

1. Integrators

   Integrators are people who let their work and life cross over, constantly blending both with lots of interruption between the two domains. They will allow work to interrupt their personal time, and likewise they attend to personal issues during work time. Let's take Susan. She works as an executive assistant for a busy high-flying executive, Katherine. When her boss calls her late in the evening saying that her flight was delayed and asking if she can book a hotel and reschedule the flights, then Susan leaps to it. And when Susan needs to leave at 4pm to be at the committee meeting for her son's soccer club, then she has the freedom to just go, no questions asked.

   In Susan's case, the work and life integration works to her advantage. She can operate more effectively in both domains by integrating the two roles. Susan is quick and fast, and typically able to jump from one task to the next without it concerning her too much. If she was the sort of person who didn't enjoy this pace and reactivity, then she may not enjoy working this way.

The challenge of this style is that you are constantly jumping from one to the other, work to non-work issues. There are fewer chunks of time where you can focus in a sustained way on either your work or non-work role. The constant switching of roles, especially if you are always reacting to crises, leads to stress and exhaustion.

But being an integrator doesn't work when the integration is not balanced. For Susan's boss Katherine, she takes calls late into the evening, works late in the office, (even sometimes around the clock), and travels at least 3 or 4 times a month away from home for business. The family issues usually come second place. Katherine was late to her daughter's high school graduation ceremony because she left it until the last minute to leave work and got stuck in traffic. She had a board meeting on the day of her father-in-law's funeral and in the rush to get from the board meeting to the funeral, forgot to pick up the flowers. In Katherine's version of integration: work first and family fits around work. But when she realised she'd let her family down, the guilt and tension made her unhappy and stressed. In the long term, her work-life integration wasn't sustainable, leading to exhaustion and burnout.

Putting the family first can also create tensions on the career side. Marina manages an all-women team of recruiters. One of her team, Anne, recently returned from maternity leave and has taken a lot of days off when the baby is sick or her childcare arrangements have fallen short. The other team members often have had to step in to cover some of the work when she is away. The other team members also have children, though some are now much older. While they had similar childcare problems they usually found other ways to cover these times so they still got into work. There is a feeling of resentment growing amongst the team members about Anne's frequent absences. This resentment is creating an unpleasant work atmosphere for Anne with her team mates.

Marina also made it quite clear to Anne that she won't be putting her forward for the next promotion. Anne is pretty upset at this as she worked hard and long hours prior to her maternity leave and feels she deserves the promotion as much as one of the other team members.

Integration is a great strategy if there is a balance so that it goes both ways: it doesn't work so well when one domain takes precedence over the other. When one area always gives, and the other always takes, it creates a role conflict. This role conflict then typically causes stress and impacts negatively on wellbeing.

2. Separators

Separators are people who try and keep the two domains, work and life, completely separate. And in certain professions it is almost impossible to do otherwise. You can't imagine a situation where an airline pilot or surgeon can suddenly stop what they are doing to take a personal call or rush to the school to pick up a sick child. But even without a job that requires a distinct separation, there are people who like to keep the two separate.

From a psychological point of view, this has the benefit of being very clear where you spend your mental energy. This is the time to focus at work, this is the time to do some exercise, this is the time to spend quality time with the family. It is a good strategy for focusing and attention – you have no interruptions from the other sphere of your life, so while at work you can focus on just work. When at home you can focus on your family or hobby.

At its extreme, then this style of managing is very rigid and not very adaptable. It is hard to always fit everything into different chunks of time. It also requires a company and a family that is prepared to accept this. For example, telling your boss you won't do an after-hours conference call with the Asian offices because it is private time, or not going to your children's sports day because it is work time can cause conflict.

3. Cyclers

Cyclers are people who focus on work for certain significant periods of time (weeks or months) and then focus on the family at other times. A classic case is someone who commutes Monday to Friday, then tries to keep the weekend completely free for family. A former colleague of mine, Freddy, does this. He flies from Zürich to London every Monday morning and back every Friday evening, while his family stays in Zürich. He tells me that the plane is like a bus, every Monday morning and Friday evening the same people are commuting to and from London and Zürich.

Freddy stayed in a cheap studio apartment with no reason to spend the evening there, it was just a place to sleep. He worked until midnight most nights of the week while he was in London so he'd be free of his work at the weekend. He was grabbing junk food for lunch and dinner and never exercising. By the time he got home for the weekend he was exhausted, getting more unfit and overweight.

He realised when he found himself breathless when playing football with his son that he had to change his lifestyle when in London, start going to the gym and eating better, otherwise he'd have a heart attack by the age of 45.

There are other roles where the work has definite peaks – the finance person who works long hours during end-of-year and month-end closing but can leave early at other times. Or the teacher who is stressed during term time, but has a longer summer holiday. The challenge is, after these peaks, if the valleys don't give you enough time to recover your energy levels. In these cases, the person feels overloaded, they feel work is still piling up and that they are slipping behind.

Work-life Integration Styles

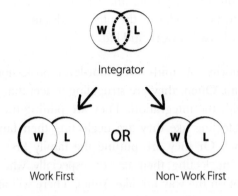

Integrator

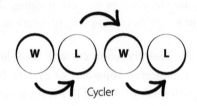

Work First   OR   Non-Work First

Cycler

Separator

Work-Life Integration Styles (from Kossek)

Whether you are an integrator, cycler or separator, one style is not better than another. It could depend on the type of work you are doing – a pilot or surgeon will have a strong separation especially when he or she is flying a plane or doing an operation. A person who spends three weeks working out on an oil rig, and two weeks at home again is going to be a cycler as the physical distance creates the boundary between work and life.

The majority of mid- to senior-level professionals are integrators. Often, they are struggling to feel that they are happy with the integration. They are putting their career first and feeling like they are neglecting their family (like Katherine). Or they are putting the family first and feel they are neglecting their career, especially when others pass them on the way up (like Anne). There will always be choices and conflicts between work and family. However, if you recognise the choices you are making, then you can change and manage your work-life integration.

 Tip 19: Identify your current work-life boundary style (integrator, separator or cycler). If you are an integrator ask yourself if it is work or non-work first. Ask if it is right for you. If you're not happy then try some of the suggestions to adjust your style.

Take Control, Set Your Own Boundaries

Looking at the different ways cyclers and separators manage their boundaries can give integrators ideas of how to manage and control their own boundaries differently. Cyclers often have a physical boundary: they are away from their normal living place, and during that time they focus on their work. Separators also may create a physical boundary: while they are at work, they work, then they mentally close the office door and come home, keeping the two places physically separate.

As an integrator, it is not so easy to keep things physically separated so that your work is only in the office and home is purely for non-work activities. It would destroy the benefits of working from home when needed and being able to sort out some personal issues while in the office. But it may still be possible to create physical boundaries within your home. For example, you could make it a rule that you only work in the study, home office or the spare bedroom. If you don't have a large space, you can keep it to one place on the dining table. You go there, get out the laptop, sit down at the desk and concentrate on the work you need to do. Then when you are finished, you are finished. You pack up or get up and leave that space. Work hasn't invaded the rest of your home.

This might seem obvious. Think about the times you've checked your smartphone while eating breakfast, on the sofa while watching TV, in the bathroom brushing your teeth... and hopefully not while you are in bed with your loved one. Your work has ended up being done everywhere from the bedroom to the bathroom and no place is sacred any more. By keeping work in one area, then when you are in the other spaces, you can enjoy relaxing, sleeping or watching TV.

To get a good night's sleep, as discussed in Chapter 3, keeping the bedroom as a sanctuary from work is a good idea on both the physical and psychological side. It is hard to go to sleep if you are thinking about work. If you create a physical space that your bedroom is only for sleep, then when you go to your bedroom, you are less likely to think about work.

Tip 20: Create physical boundaries in your home where you work and where you don't.

And it is not just space in the home. Some people also separate by having two phones, their work phone and their personal phone. With a second non-work phone, you can keep in touch with people but at a time you've designated as non-work; that way, you're not going to see a little red number showing the number of work emails in your inbox. It can be a bit clunky and confusing for your contacts who fall into both work and friend categories. On the other hand, it does allow you to put the work phone away, and not be tempted by the alerts and rising red number to get sucked back into work.

Time is a boundary for cyclers. While it might be impossible for you to say you never work after hours or at the weekend, there is a big difference in being available all the time at the weekend and in the evenings. Checking an email quickly here and there over the weekend might feel efficient, but it is the switching that is draining. I recall going skiing on a Saturday. It was a fantastic day, sunny, blue sky and beautiful scenery. I was feeling on top of the world after a great day out. On the trip home from the ski area, it seemed like a waste of time just sitting on the train, so I got out the work phone and there was an email with some bad news about one of our top staff being poached by one of our competitors. Suddenly, the pleasure of the day was gone, and not coming back. After discussions with my coach I made a rule for myself: no checking emails until Sunday evening. For me it was important to have one day of the week when I could mentally switch off and really enjoy life.

I had a boss, Jake, who constantly sent emails throughout the weekend. He told us he was using his "wasted time" when he had to drive his teenage kids to weekend sports. He would sit on the sidelines writing and answering emails on his phone. For work purposes, it wasn't ideal as often his emails were very short and cryptic, and I'm sure he spent more time explaining something again later. I'm not sure it was good for his family. To this day I've wondered how his kids felt about their dad who seemed to be more interested in his phone than watching them play sport.

 Tip 21: Create time boundaries between home and work. Choose when you will work over the weekend – you don't have to be on call 24/7.

Physical boundaries and time boundaries are one way of you controlling the demarcation between your work and life. Psychological boundaries are another way, where you try not to think about work during your personal time or vice versa. It is about mentally switching off from work so that thoughts about your upcoming presentation or next big project don't fill your head during your non-work time when you should be enjoying being with your family, friends or doing a hobby. On the other side, likewise when you've had an argument with your partner or are worried about a sick friend, you can find you're thinking about this at work, suddenly missing the important point of a meeting.

Creating psychological boundaries is hard. If I say don't think about a big hairy gorilla then instantly a thought of a big hairy gorilla jumps into your mind. Mindfulness and meditation are two ways already discussed for focusing your thoughts on the here and now, being present and trying to enjoy things now, not worrying about the future or the past. Unlike my workaholic boss writing emails instead of watching his kids play sport, mindfulness would recommend that he enjoy watching his kids, enjoy being outside on a nice day (though perhaps some days it isn't so nice to be standing around in the cold and wet). Then to be present and fully concentrated on his work during the work period.

Holidays especially seem to be a challenge – should you disconnect and enjoy a chance to wind down and relax, but come back to an inbox of a thousand emails? Or is it better to deal with emails as they come in while you are on holiday? If you can't turn off the emails during the vacation, then set aside a time when you deal with them, say between 5pm and 6pm every evening. And then spend the rest of the time enjoying yourself. Do not spend your time on the beach checking emails between dips in the sea and sunbathing. The psychological drain will make you feel like you've not had a real vacation.

There are also times where you can create buffer zones that will help you transition from work to home and back again. A buffer zone allows you to process the day and put some of it behind you. The commute is one of those times you could use to slowly start switching off from work. For many people, the commute has become a time that is now an extension of working time to answer a few emails, to make phone calls as you are driving home. That means when you arrive home, you are still in work thinking mode.

I'm sure you can recognise it in your partner when they've had a bad day at work, even if you don't notice it in yourself. Your partner comes in the door and suddenly you get a complete data dump about their terrible day at work. They are still processing what has happened and trying to make sense of it. This working through the day at work and reflecting can be productive if it is structured. Ask yourself what went well, what not so well and what I would do differently next time. This gives time to calm down the thoughts and switch to a different channel, the non-work channel. Switching off and switching on to the next phase of the day is easier with some head space. A buffer zone like listening to music or the radio while driving, getting some exercise by walking or biking to work or even reading a book or just daydreaming on the train are good ways to create a buffer zone. It is more energising than jumping straight from one busy day at work to a busy non-work activity.

 Tip 22: Create psychological boundaries and buffer zones between work and home so you can mentally switch off work when not working and vice-versa.

These may not be big changes to your work and life integration, but the feeling that you are the one in control and are consciously making the choice is important. It is far more stressful to feel you "**have** to answer that work email" or "**have** to pick up the kids". If you have made the choice that you will integrate work and life, then it is not that you **have** to it, but it is your **choice** to do it and when you do it.

 Tip 23: Take control of your boundaries and decide when and how you will integrate your work and life. Don't just let it happen.

Learning to Say No

Putting yourself in control means that sometimes you just say "no". There are too many things to do, that should be done, must be done, you're expected to do, have to get done.

Most of us don't like to be seen to be letting someone down, to be not pulling our weight or not doing some of the things we "should do" or "ought to do". But to manage work-life integration, sometimes you should say no, and stick firmly to your time scheduling.

Some people find it really hard to say no. They are the ones asked to do every piece of extra work, to be on every committee and always available to help. Some people just give too much of their time and energy to others, not realising that it means that they will burn out. Burnout was originally studied, over 40 years ago, in professions like social workers and teachers, where they gave a lot of their energy to helping people, sometime successfully but also sometimes not. Over time, they became exhausted, cynical and felt they were no longer effective or improving.

Burnout is a phrase now used in other professions, and in our highly collaborative and matrixed organisations, there are ad hoc requests coming from all quarters. Burnout comes from trying to help everyone in the organisation whenever they request it – or sometimes even when they don't ask for it. Like Penny, a participant in a workshop I ran on attention management. At the start of the session, we did the usual introduction round and I asked the participants to make a comment about what their specific challenge was around managing their attention. The first participant introduced himself and said the issue he was struggling with was finding time to write his novel while working full time. Penny jumped in and started giving suggestions on how he could set aside time (while I was thinking "Hey! I'm the facilitator of this course!"). Then the same thing happened after the next person explained their challenge and so on around the room. Finally, it came to Penny's turn and her issue, not surprisingly, was that she was always being pulled away from her work to help her colleagues.

I wondered just how much her colleagues did ask Penny to help and whether she actually volunteered in the same way she'd just demonstrated in the workshop. It was as if she couldn't help herself from taking over and solving other people's problems. I could see how being too helpful and too eager to give advice Penny was ending up with more and more work. I'm sure it made her feel a useful and valued part of the team, but also extremely busy.

I'm not suggesting that you become the office grouch, the one your colleagues avoid at all costs because you are so unhelpful. However, if you always put your colleagues' requests before your own job responsibilities, even placing your family before your own needs for relaxation, then you will eventually burn out. It is flattering to be the one who is always asked – you feel clever, important, indispensable. It's great to share your knowledge and help. But resist the temptation to take over. People will learn more if they do it themselves. And you can say no nicely by reframing it so you are first being positive before saying no[58]. Be careful to avoid starting off apologetically, or you'll probably get talked back into it.

 Tip 24: Learn to say no nicely by reframing it in a positive way and offering an alternative.

1. Start with a comment that you are happy they asked.

2. Explain in a positive way that you have another major priority.

3. Then you can be apologetic.

4. Try to help with an alternative suggestion of who could help or what you could offer instead.

LEARN TO SAY NO NICELY
If you hate saying no then try

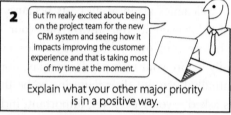

Saying No Nicely

Take Control

Technology has slowly invaded every corner of our castle, bringing work into every time, space and place, both physically and psychologically. The dark side of flexible working is that it can become all pervasive, taking over your every waking moment. To manage effectively, you need be the one taking control by creating boundaries, physically and psychologically, with your space and time. Don't let technology, work or family demands control you. You decide when you want to switch on and off the phone and your thoughts about work.

Chapter Recap

- *Identify your current work-life boundary style (integrator, separator or cycler). If you are an integrator ask yourself if it is work or non-work first. Ask if it is right for you. If you're not happy then try some of the suggestions to adjust your style.*

- *Create physical boundaries in your home separating where you work and where you don't.*

- *Create time boundaries between home and work. Choose when and if you will work over the weekend – you don't have to be on call 24/7.*

- *Create psychological boundaries and buffer zones between work and home so you can mentally switch off work thoughts and concerns when not working, and vice-versa.*

- *Take control of your boundaries and decide when and how you will integrate your work and life. Don't just let it happen.*

- *Learn to say no nicely by reframing it in a positive way and offering an alternative.*

CHAPTER 6:

Change and Making It Stick

> Every human being has the freedom to change at any instance.
>
> - Viktor Frankl

If you are the sort of person who is very self-controlled and strong-willed and you always stick to a healthy diet, exercise regularly, get plenty of sleep and never allow yourself to be distracted, then you are most welcome to skip this chapter (or in fact maybe this entire book). This chapter is for the rest of us normal people.

Whether it is managing boundaries between work and life, or getting back into a stress-relieving activity like exercise or meditation, these are new behaviours you can learn and practice. New behaviours will take time and energy to become a regular part of your routine, to become part of your habits. To become a new habit, it requires changing from the way you do things now to a new way, not just once, but frequently so it is part of your regular pattern.

There are a few ways that you can help yourself to make the change easier.

Just Do It

One of the hardest things to do can be to actually start it. The first step is the easiest to put off. It is not a coincidence that Nike's motto is "Just do it" to motivate people to get into sport and fitness (while wearing Nike gear of course!). Most New Year's resolutions are broken within five weeks[59]. The beginning is often harder than we imagine. It takes time and energy to change our patterns and habits that have formed over several years. Expecting them to change overnight is setting yourself a very high expectation.

The procrastinator's motto is the opposite of Nike's: it is "just put it off until tomorrow". Nobody plans on being a procrastinator. But our intrinsic reward system is set up to reward us with short-term gratification instead of long term goals that are some way off. Tim Urban describes procrastination cleverly in his blog[60] and TED talk[61], how he managed to procrastinate so much that a thesis he had a year to complete was left unstarted until just 24 hours before the deadline.

Tim describes his brain as being ruled by his Instant Gratification Monkey rather than his rational brain. The rational part of the brain knows that he should start his thesis. But the Instant Gratification Monkey takes over with any excuse to avoid starting the thesis. As the monkey's name so aptly describes, procrastination leaves us feeling temporarily happy – we've done something much more fun than the thesis or whatever we should be doing.

Then Tim describes the Panic Monster, the feeling when he realises that the deadline is fast approaching and now he must work like crazy to make up for lost time. The Panic Monster kicks in huge amounts of stress hormones, launches him into a fit of energetic but unstructured work on his thesis. He gets his thesis in by the deadline, but naturally, it was not of the quality that would have been achieved with a year's work instead of 24 hours' work. Even a genius is unlikely to be able to pull that off.

Panic Monster   Instant Gratification Monkey

Procrastination (from Tim Urban)

The panic also has a negative effect on your health as your stress levels rocket through the roof. Procrastinating college students, in one semester, had more colds, bouts of flu and gastrointestinal problems and suffered from higher levels of insomnia than their non-procrastinating peers[62].

The internet is the procrastinator's playground. It can look and feel like you are working while you are surfing the internet. You can start off with needing to know something slightly relevant to your work, let's say, a fact about marine life in the Amazon river, which can lead you, after a few minutes to the Amazon book store. There, you start browsing interesting books, then end up watching a Leonardo DiCaprio video about deforestation in the Amazon, and finally checking out an interview with Leonardo's mother on the *Oprah Winfrey Show*.

We can still procrastinate even without the internet by idly wandering around a shopping mall, or sitting in a park and chatting to strangers or reading a magazine. Then you'd feel like you are wasting time so you don't go out to the shop or the park or pick up a magazine. Conversely, the internet feels like work and the non-work stuff is so much more interesting than the work you are supposed to do. Suddenly an hour has gone by without you even noticing. Your Instant Gratification Monkey is happy but your rational brain is not. So, if there is something you really need to do and you want to do it, then you must push aside your Instant Gratification Monkey, think about all the rational benefits and just get started.

 Tip 25: Just do it. The first step is the hardest so the most important thing is just to get started.

Try Anything Not Just Once, But Two or Three Times

My father has an appalling joke I've heard far too many times in my life. "I read a book once, didn't like it, so never read another one". For the record, my father has read many books in his life but the point is that you can't try something only once to decide if you like it or not. A friend of mine said something similar about yoga. "I went to a yoga class a few years ago. I found it too slow and boring. It's not for me." Yoga classes, like books, come in many different types, styles and speeds. So, trying one class is like reading one book and saying you'll never read another. It might be worth trying a different yoga school.

For any of the tips in this book you might have to try several different types until you find the one that suits you. For example, the tip that recommends doing more exercise to relieve stress, you first need to find the type of exercise that you want to do – jogging, swimming, walking, going to the gym. For me, it's jogging outside in the fresh air (and hopefully sunshine). I enjoy and find it stress-relieving. However it is not so inspiring to go out in the middle of a dark, cold winter's night when there is snow and ice around. Instead there's the gym. You might need to try a few different types of exercise to find the one that you enjoy, fits in with your lifestyle and even the different seasons.

Carrying on with the analogy of reading a book, you also must learn to read first before you'll enjoy reading a book. You know if you've helped a child to learn to read that they can get frustrated if the book is too difficult. It's too slow, too many words they don't know and it soon gets tedious. For children, we make it easier by starting with shorter books, teaching them to read and reading them stories. Slowly, slowly improving, starting with picture books, until years later, moving to great books like *War and Peace*.

As adults, we seem to forget there is a learning phase, and expect to be able to try something once and be reasonably good at it. If you have not run for years, then the first time that you try, you will probably feel unfit, out of breath and uncomfortable. After a few more times it will get better, you'll get fitter, more into the rhythm and start enjoying it more. The saying "it's just like riding a bike", meaning that you'll never forget how to do something you learned as a child has some truth, but is not the whole truth. Yes, your body remembers how to balance on a bicycle, but that doesn't mean that the first time you get back on a bicycle after a few years that you'll not have some sore muscles, especially if you start off with 100 kilometres and lots of hills.

Some of the tips around mindset are literally harder to "get your head around". There is not a screen on our forehead showing us, and others, what we are thinking. If you are feeling very stressed, someone who is close to you might recognise the signs, for example you're snappy and irritable, or not sleeping well, or forgetful and preoccupied. While someone else can help you with advice, counselling or coaching, in the end **you** are the only person who can change the way you are thinking about something. Shifting your mindset, reframing your thinking, calming your thought patterns with meditation – just like physical changes – takes time and practice. And, like physical change, the first couple of times it will feel uncomfortable and unnatural. Keep trying to reframe your thinking and try a new activity more than once.

But not everything will work for everyone. At some point, you might just say you've tried but it is not your thing. Cross-fit is the latest fitness trend that everyone is raving about. But perhaps you don't find it relaxing. The noise and competition is too much. After trying it two to three times, then you can decide if it is for you or not.

 Tip 26: Try these tips or something new two to three times before you decide if you like it or not. Remember that you will have to learn some skills first that take time and feel uncomfortable at the beginning.

Make it a Habit

Now you've got started and tried it two to three times and know you like it, how do you make it something that you integrate into your everyday life so it improves the way you're working and living? While bad habits can be difficult to break, forming new habits is harder. If you understand what helps keep you motivated, supported and committed, then you've got more chance of achieving your goal.

I'm sure you've seen clips of coaches giving a pep talk to their teams, and they finish off with a hip-hurrah and lots of high fives. The pep talk often involves the coach making sure that the team are very clear about their goal, but also often encourages them to imagine what it will feel like to win the game. Imagining their feelings of pride, elation and joy creates a powerful driver to play their heart out in the game.

Try creating an image in your mind of what it will look like when you reach your goal. Is it a serene and calm space, a weekend to yourself, or a vision of a less stressed version of yourself where you are enjoying life and work? Maybe it is looking forward to work instead of dragging yourself out of bed with a sense of dread and foreboding. Perhaps it is finding time to exercise away your stress at the end of a busy work day.

This technique is called Goal Imagery[63], and for it to work, you need to imagine your goal in some detail with all your senses. You think about how it will feel when you've achieved it, but also visualise what it will look like, perhaps how it will sound (e.g. the cheers from a crowd), even how it will taste or smell. Remember how it felt on one occasion when you were feeling good, enjoying work and life, perhaps just after a successful presentation. Remember not just how it felt but what were the sounds, smells, the taste of success. Use this strong image to motivate yourself towards your goals.

You can break them down into short, medium and long-term goals and select an image for each of them. Imagine if you could be so much more focused at work that you could leave the office 20 minutes earlier each day. What would that look like, the calm of not rushing to the childcare centre just a couple of minutes before the official closing time, worrying if you will be fined again? Then if you were 30 minutes earlier out of work, you would have the time to get your running shoes on and head for a short walk after work on a lovely summer's evening. And long-term, if there was another hour in your day, what a calm relaxing evening would look like.

Some people even like to find a picture or a series of pictures from magazines, or create a vision board on Pinterest that illustrates their goal. If you're a visual person, it can be very helpful to make this clear in a visual way. For others, it can be a song that reminds them of a special time or makes them feel good. And when you feel yourself slipping back into the old routines (more on that to come) you can have a look at your pin board or play the song and get some renewed energy from imagining what it will be like to achieve your goal.

 Tip 27: Use goal imagery to create a vision of what it will feel like, look like (even smell and taste) when you've achieved your goal and imagine this when you are needing to get motivated.

There are two ways of starting something new, which are analogous to how people might enter a cold swimming pool. Some people take a short run and jump straight into the water, getting a huge initial shock, gasping for breath as the cold hits them. But then they are in, and they adjust to the temperature. Other people stand on the edge slowly tiptoeing their way into the water, inch by inch. They very slowly get acclimatised and then eventually they are in the water and swimming around.

When it comes to forming a new habit, people often think they must take the first approach, jumping straight into the deep end. And for some people it works; after the initial shock they adjust and get used to it. It can be like the first morning at boot camp at the military, with the rough shock of multiple routines changing all at once; getting up time, different food, new regime and a bossy sergeant. The problem is that the shock of hitting the cold water can be so unpleasant that you don't want to do it again – ever.

Starting Slowly or Leaping in at the Deep End

The gradual adjustment of inching slowly into the cold water can also work. If you want to change something, then start with the really small steps that help build the routine. For example, if you decide you are going to start running before work, you need to get up a half an hour earlier to fit it in. The first morning your goal is just to get up and put your running clothes on, but not actually go out for a run. I can hear you already saying, "Now that sounds a bit stupid, once you've got your running clothes on, you may as well get out there and at least go for a walk." Exactly! This is likely to motivate you to at least start developing the routine of getting up a little earlier. From there you build on it and it starts to become a part of your normal behaviour and finally a habit[64].

Just as you wouldn't expect to be able to run a marathon without training, then you can't change the habit of checking and responding to your emails every 5 minutes during your evening and weekends. But you can set yourself the goal of ignoring your emails for an hour, then slowly you can build up to longer. If you want to start meditating, then starting with 10 minutes is more realistic than trying an hour.

The whole-hearted leap from the side of the pool in the cold water can work, and is especially effective to get quick results. If you want to lose weight and go off to a health farm for a month where only healthy food is served, and offering you a wide range of daily exercise classes, you will find a quick improvement. But when you get home, you need to keep up the healthy eating and exercise routine which is suddenly much harder with the other demands and pressures around you. If you really want to change, you should gradually make it part of your life routines.

Tip 28: Start with small steps, even really tiny, tiny little steps.

I possibly shouldn't admit this but one thing that I discovered when coaching is how much progress people make towards their goal because they feel they need to report back to me by the next session. I'm not their boss, I'm not their mother, their partner and not any kind of judge or jury. The goals are their own, goals they know they want to achieve having spent some time discussing with me. Of course, I'd like to think it is my deep knowledge of psychology and the profound questions that I ask (and seriously, I hope these do play a part). The reality is, if you are clear on your goal, and you feel you should report back to someone, then you are much more likely to do it.

The first step of telling the goal to someone else helps make the goal clearer. Something that is an idea in your mind is not a clear goal. When you articulate it to someone else, you start to clarify it. They might challenge you if it is unrealistic and suggest how you could make it work better.

Once the goal is clear, it is out there. Then the second step of having someone to show some accountability to (whether it is a coach, a friend or a family member), can help make a goal happen. Then once the goal is clear, it is easy to agree how you will commit to it. If you tell your partner you are committed to keeping Saturday free from work so you have some time to switch off over the weekend, if your partner sees you checking an email, you'll realise you need to question your own motives without him or her needing to say anything.

In a group coaching session that I facilitate, I have seen how important it is to note down what people say they will do and ask them to report back at the next session in a month's time. The following session, we start by reviewing these plans or goals; it makes the person want to reach them, or at least have made some progress. It is why groups like Weight Watchers or Alcoholics Anonymous can work to support behavioural change. Maybe there is a group of "Smartphone Addicted Workaholics Anonymous" that you can join? But seriously, tell your colleagues at work that you are trying to balance work and life by focusing better at work, and this will encourage you to show them you are working on it.

 Tip 29: Build in the commitment to your goal with an accountability partner.

We love to feel like we are achieving something. In Chapter 4 we talked about the buzz you get when you see progress. Teresa Amabile[65] researched over 200 people in seven companies to answer the question about what made them more productive at work. She found that clear goals and making progress towards the goal made people motivated and engaged.

When you set a goal for yourself, you need to see the progress towards that goal. If it is measurable then that is easy – a few hours without digital distraction, or so many exercise sessions a week. Some things are harder to measure, like feeling less stressed. But this is where keeping a journal can help. Note down how you are feeling at the end of the day, the level of stress you've experienced. Looking back over the week you can then see a pattern and progress.

Tip 30: Measure the progress of advancement towards your goal. If it is not easy to measure, then note how you feel in a journal.

Slipping Out of Habits

The challenge with any new behaviour is that it is easy to fall back into old patterns. The important thing is that what you do when you slip out of a new habit is not to punish yourself, but accept that you are a fallible human being and that means you are not perfect[66].

This is easier said than done if you are a typical high achiever. High achievers set high standards for themselves (and others) and work hard to live up to them. This keeps them motivated and driven. But the dark side is they take fall backs very hard, and often drive themselves even harder, creating stress for themselves. They look at an achievement as not quite good enough. Instead of congratulating themselves on trying to learn meditation, they tell themselves it wasn't good enough, that they are hopeless at it because they didn't pick it up fast enough.

If you were constantly being told by a friend that you aren't good enough, then after a while you'd soon realise they are not a good friend. A good friend would give you constructive, helpful advice that encourages you to keep going. However, often it is our own inner thoughts that are criticising us in a way we would never do to a good friend. We need to be like a friend to ourselves, not judge ourselves so harshly when we have fallen back.

When you set yourself a goal, be proud and happy when you are making progress. When you slip back don't tell yourself off. Accept that it happens to the best of us and the important thing is how you keep moving on towards your goal again.

 Tip 31: Accept that you will slip back from time to time, and move on again.

Change of Habit and the Habit of Change

The challenge of any book that offers advice and tips, is that people read it but don't apply what they have read to change the way they are living and working. We are very complex creatures and changing the way you've been thinking and behaving is not easy. If you're used to working till midnight every night and then you suddenly stop work at 6 pm, you'll feel strange, odd and uncomfortable, even if it is giving up something unpleasant. Trying to learn a new pattern, behaviour or mindset takes energy and attention, and it can be more stressful at the start than doing things the same old way. But breaking out of the pattern or that rut is essential to move forward and make changes.

So just do it, but also just do it two to three times because the first time you try anything new, you probably won't like it. Then set a clear goal, imagine yourself achieving it, start off with really tiny steps with the support of an accountability partner, and then feel the buzz of progress. This is not a quick-fix wonder-cure that will guarantee change overnight, but it will help change to happen.

Chapter Recap

- *Just do it. The first step is the hardest so the most important thing is just to get started.*

- *Try these tips or something new two to three times before you decide if you like it or not. Remember that you will have to learn some skills first that take time and feel uncomfortable at first.*

- *Use goal imagery to create a vision of what it will feel like, look like (even smell and taste like) when you've achieved your goal, and imagine this when you are needing to get motivated.*

- *Start with small steps, even really tiny, tiny little steps.*

- *Build in the commitment to your goal with an accountability partner.*

- *Measure the progress of advancement towards your goal. If it is not easy to measure then note how you feel in a journal.*

- *Accept that you will slip back from time to time, and move on again.*

CHAPTER 7:

Crazy Cultures and Toxic Workplaces

Life in the fast lane
surely make you lose your mind

Life in the fast lane
everything all the time

- The Eagles, 1976. Joe Walsh, Glenn Frey and Don Henley

Most of this book has been focused on you and what you can do to change the way you are thinking, acting and behaving. But sometimes it is not all about you. Rather it's the external factors, some of them outside your control, that are having an impact on concentration at work. You might need to question the organisational culture, the leadership behaviour, your job requirements or if the organisational set-up is the right one for you. There could be a point where you realise that perhaps this is not the organisation for you – how they work, what they are doing is not the way that suits your way of working. Always being the square peg in the round hole doesn't make you motivated and focused.

The Crazy-Busy Culture

It becomes almost a badge of honour to answer anyone who asks, "How are you?" with the reply "Oh busy, crazy-busy". To not tell everyone that you are busy would almost be sacrilege in this fast-paced world. If you are not busy it means you haven't got an important job, an active social life or enough outside work activities[67]. And not just at work, but on the weekend – if you can't return to the office with either a tale about the mountains you've climbed or the marathon you've run, then you are just not getting enough out of life. To say you spent the weekend attending to household chores or going to the movies is just not going to sound significant to some of your highly competitive colleagues.

The organisational culture, the way that our leaders behave, the way our colleagues behave can start affecting the way we think about work and what is "normal". It took me a while to realise it, but at one of the organisations that I worked in, the leadership did not set a very good example as to how to balance their work and life. I had one boss, Katherine (I mentioned her a couple times before) who was constantly rushing from one meeting to another, taking calls early hours and late into the night. She was a real night owl and would work on something and send emails at very late hours, often well after midnight.

If I woke up and started the morning reading her emails, it felt worse to me than having a cold shower. I had to learn to be disciplined enough not to start reading my emails before arriving at the office, otherwise my working day would start from the minute I checked them. To be fair, she didn't expect us to be working through the night too and she was not the type that expected emails to be answered within an hour of being sent, but she did not set a good example of work-life balance.

In the same company, I had another boss, Jake, (yes two bosses – oh, the joys of the matrix organisation!) who sent a lot of emails on the weekend (I mentioned him in Chapter 5 – the one doing his emails while the kids were playing sport). Based on my experience with Katherine, I didn't imagine that Jake was expecting me to respond over the weekend, but I'd never actually asked. Another colleague on the management team was concerned that she wasn't meeting his expectations and asked me about it. We'd just finished a management meeting and were about to have a management team dinner. We agreed to put the question to Jake in front of the whole team. Jake explained he preferred to use his time over the weekend to send a few emails when he had some down time. He didn't expect us to answer emails over the weekend. If there was something urgent he needed to speak to us about over the weekend, then he would send us a text message or phone us.

The important point was that we asked what was expected of us. Fortunately, Katherine and Jake's expectations were reasonable and we knew we weren't expected to be available every weekend. But somehow it was just part of the way things were done in that company, not just by Jake and Katherine but nearly all the senior managers. It was part of the culture to work long hours and to be available at all hours. It gave those of us one rung lower in the organisation the impression that the only way to get to the top was to do the same – sacrifice family, fitness, sleep and health. And it seems to be a common experience as 41% surveyed in the UK believe that to progress at their workplace, they usually have to put in long hours.[68]

Other stories I have heard regarding the expectations of certain organisations' managers are not reasonable. A client told me about a manager who would comment when anyone in the team left the office about 7pm in the evening, "Taking a half day today are you?" The manager had also admonished my client for having his mobile turned off one evening while he was at a concert. He hadn't replied to a message his boss sent about 8pm until he got home nearly 4 hours later.

Fortunately, most leaders are not quite that extreme. Still, as a leader in an organisation, it is important to think about the example that you could be setting for your team. I was surprised to learn after a few laughs over some drinks that my team also thought that I was some crazy, super-career woman who enjoyed working all hours. One of my team had a baby and so I had knitted a little baby jacket. It was a look of genuine shock and surprise when I gave it to her and she said, *"You knitted it, how did you find the time?"* because she just couldn't imagine me sitting in front of the TV knitting. Another time a colleague told me off for calling into a management team meeting while I was on holiday. He told me I was setting an example that he'd be forced to follow next time he was on holiday at the time of a management meeting.

It is easy to get sucked into a vortex of working long hours if it is part of the culture, and start to believe it is the only way to get to the top. Instead, challenge the assumption, clarify the expectations and make sure you are setting a good role model for your team.

Tip 32: Clarify the expectations from your bosses of the hours they expect you to work, especially around answering out-of-hours and weekend emails. You hopefully are pleasantly surprised that they aren't expecting an answer immediately.

A Game of Thrones – Office Politics in Uncertain Times

While my old company had some dark days, and expected a lot from their staff, there are organisations that are much worse. There are places where the office politics look like an episode from *Game of Thrones*, where bullying goes on, with lots of people getting stabbed in the back, as people make power plays based on their self-interest and self-promotion. Often this environment goes hand-in-hand with times that are uncertain and people are under the threat of redundancy. There is nothing like fighting for a limited number of positions that makes people turn against each other.

In these environments, the hours that you are working are under much more scrutiny. The answering of emails at all hours becomes proof that you are dedicated and hard working. In a survey of 1000 UK workers, over half admitted to doing "competitive overtime", that is staying later in the office than colleagues to impress their boss. A third admitted to sending emails after hours to impress their boss. Then really sinking to lowest levels of sucking up, 12% admitted they sent pointless emails when they were working from home, and 4% said they set up their email scheduler to send emails to impress their boss[69]. Perhaps it's time to ask yourself why you are sending those out-of-hours emails – because it is critical to get the work done, or because you want to impress your boss?

If your answer is to impress your boss, then this is an interesting realisation. It might be part of the game that you have to play in a competitive and insecure job environment. Then it may be time to ask yourself if it is the sort of environment that you want to work in, long term. These toxic workplaces don't help your productivity or that of your team members and colleagues.

 Tip 33: Think about why you are sending emails out-of-hours, and stop the ones that are just for sucking up.

Google are the masters of our current universe of data, so not surprisingly they have spent time looking at quantitative data as to why some teams work together well, and some do not. The reason some teams work better than others, is psychological safety.

Psychological safety is the opposite to the *Game of Thrones* culture. Psychological safety describes the feeling that you can trust the other team members. You feel happy to ask a question and not worry that the other person might think you're not up with the play. You feel free to suggest a new idea, even if it is a little crazy and "out there". Without psychological safety, then people are carefully monitoring what they are saying, thinking about the politics and not working for the team goal. The research identified four other factors, that all built on psychological safety[70].

Sinking several levels below this ideal psychologically safe team are environments where incivility, rudeness and bullying is tolerated by the leaders, or is the behaviour of the leaders. These sorts of workplaces are described as toxic workplaces and are run by leaders called toxic bosses.

In these environments, no one feels safe and productivity declines. The team members are less willing to point out mistakes or suggest improvements and become emotionally exhausted. People who work with a leader who respects them are more productive and engaged compared to one who is rude, uncivil and difficult[71].

Top five factors for effective team work:

1. Psychological safety: Can we take risks in this team without feeling insecure or embarrassed?

2. Dependability: Can we count on each other to do high quality work on time?

3. Structure and clarity: Are goals, roles, and execution of plans for our team clear?

4. Meaning of work: Are we working on something that is personally important to each of us?

5. Impact of work: Do we fundamentally believe that the work we're doing matters?

If you answered "yes" to all 5 of these questions then yes, you should be working in a high performing team.

And if you are surrounded by rude, selfish people then you will start to act like that yourself – even though normally you are a cooperative helpful person. People who come from a supportive, friendly environment are more likely to help someone else, even if they see no pay-off. Their natural reaction is to help because they see that they have benefited from someone else's generosity in the past. They are happy to pay it forward. If you work in a highly political

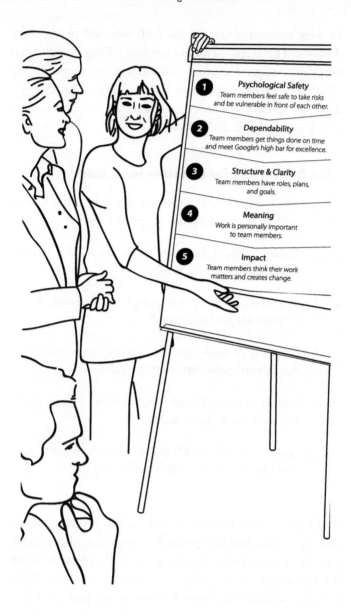

Five Factors for Effective Teams (from Google)

environment, then you stop to think about whether you should help someone first and it curbs your natural instinct to be helpful. After a while people stop helping each other at all, even when it would pay off, because it has become their normal behaviour[72].

Finding Your Purpose in Work

Since the 2008 stock market crash, the failure of many reputable banks and various corporate scandals, people are questioning the values of organisations they work for. At a personal level, this is a crisis of conscience where people want to do something they feel has a real purpose and is adding value to the community, society or the wide world. They can see the impact of their work, not just within the organisation but also that the work their organisation does has a purpose, it strives to be a force for good in the world, not just making money for the shareholders.

Even with the right environment, there can be organisations where what they do just doesn't excite and enthuse you. You should feel that what you are doing for the majority of your days is contributing value to the world in a way that you also see as valuable. Without this, it is hard to be motivated and engaged. That doesn't mean that we all chuck in our jobs and go to work for the United Nations or Save the Children Fund. But if there is alignment between what we believe in, and the purpose and values of the organisation we work for, then it is easier to get excited about and engaged in our work.

I worked for a short period of time for a company that ran drug trials. This is hugely important work in helping find cures for all sorts of currently incurable diseases, from cancer to Parkinson's disease. There was a noble purpose. But once I understood the business model, the execution felt to me to be very exploitative and I had a hard time reconciling this with my values. The company ran drug trials in Eastern Europe and Russia. They operated in these countries because it was easier to motivate the patients to be involved in a drug trial. The doctor's recommendation to be involved in a trial was seen as unbiased, the patients had fewer other options for treatment and the payment they received (equivalent of 1000 Euros) went further than in western countries. I felt there was something exploitative about the business and the company owners were getting very wealthy. For me, I found if I didn't believe in what the company was doing, then it was hard to get motivated about my work.

I'm sure you've looked at other people and their jobs and thought "I wouldn't last a week doing that job," even if it is noble, worthy and fulfilling to them. It is important to recognise what your purpose is and find a job or organisation that helps you achieve your purpose. Aaron Hurst[73] spent some time thinking deeply about purpose and how people will be more effective in whatever they do if they align to their sense of purpose. He suggested there are three questions to ask yourself to try and identify your purpose at work – who we serve, how we serve them and why we serve them.

Do you want to have an impact on

- individuals
- organisations
- whole society

- What is your reason for wanting to have an impact?
- What are the values or moral compass underlying why you do something?

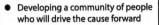

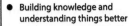

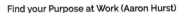

- Developing a community of people who will drive the cause forward
- Building knowledge and understanding things better
- Improving processes and policies
- Tapping into the people and using their ideas.

Find your Purpose at Work (Aaron Hurst)

If you're doing a job for the money, the status or because you feel you have no other options, then it is hard to be intrinsically motivated and focused.

 Tip 34: Find an organisation where you are aligned to the purpose, believe in what, how and why they do it, you'll find it easier to focus. Time will fly and you'll probably fly with it.

Finding Utopia

Change or leave may be the two options you're left with if you are in the wrong organisation. Ideally, you could alter part of your job, manage your stress levels better, challenge your boss appropriately, reframe your thinking or set clearer boundaries. But sometimes it is not all about you, it is them. You can't change the whole organisation's culture, fire your toxic boss or direct the organisation's strategy to align with your sense of purpose. Then it's time to admit you're the one that should move on – you are the square peg. Before you do move on to somewhere else, it is good to be clear about what you are looking for. Utopia will be impossible to find but somewhere closer to utopia is worth searching for.

It can be hard to find the perfect place where you get it all aligned between culture, leadership, team and purpose. It's like finding the perfect partner, perfect holiday or perfect house. The first step would be to understand what you are looking for as the perfect job. You can assess this using the questionnaire in the appendix. There are probably some compromises that you are going to have to make. The worst house in the best street, but hopefully you'll be able to renovate it to make it better. You can think about finding the perfect job in that way too. It really is hard to find but you might be able to adjust something to make it better.

The issue can be that it is hard to tell what the job is like until you are in it. So how do you go and find out more? There may be someone you know who also works there, or sources of information on the internet (e.g. Glassdoor). It is not diplomatic or a good move to ask if your boss is toxic or if you'll be expected to work unreasonable hours, or if the work environment is like an episode from the *Game of Thrones*. You can find some suggestions in the appendix.

Life in the Organisational Vortex

Organisational culture, the way things are done in a company, creates its own norms and standards. They become so accepted that you don't question why you are doing things – why you are working late, answering emails at all hours. It's easy to get sucked into the organisational vortex and being like the worst version of yourself – selfish, sucking up and working like a maniac.

It takes a courageous person to be brave enough to rebel against the norms, or to start asking a boss who works all the weekend whether he or she expects his team to do the same. The invasion of work-life boundaries is relatively new and organisations need to learn how to manage it. Discussing this topic is not part of the normal conversation held in an organisation. Challenging norms requires a gentle rebellion to contest how things are done at your place of work, and to set a positive role model for your team.

Then it can take a lot of courage to realise that you are in the wrong organisation, perhaps a toxic workplace or where the values and purpose of the organisation are not aligned with your values or sense of purpose. In these circumstances, it might take realising that the career that you have fought for is not the dream after all. Utopia is hard to find, but sometimes moving on somewhere else is the only option.

Chapter Recap

- *Clarify the expectations from your bosses of the hours they expect you to work, especially around answering out-of-hours and weekend emails. You hopefully are pleasantly surprised that they aren't expecting an answer immediately.*

- *Think about why you are sending emails out of hours, and stop the ones that are just for sucking up.*

- *Find an organisation where you are aligned to the purpose, believe in what, how and why they do it, you'll find it easier to focus. Time will fly and you'll probably fly with it.*

CONCLUSION:

Focus at Work, Switch Off, Enjoy Life

Life is what happens while you are busy making other plans.

- John Lennon

The world has got faster, busier and more stressful without us even noticing it. It crept up on us slowly. It's only when we start comparing our current situation with our work-life balance 15 or 20 years ago that we realise how much things have changed. And it's not just how much "things" have changed but also, unwittingly, how we have changed too: what we are now prepared to accept, how we behave, when we work and how focused (or unfocused) we are when we are working.

Technology is a key factor in this, but more importantly, it is how we choose to deal with the technology that impacts our work and life. With smartphones, laptops, tablets and wifi everywhere, it means we can be accessible 24/7. We choose whether we are accessible 24/7 or not. There are some reasonable boundaries that you can draw between work and life that will make you handle work better and enjoy your life more.

Whether you decide that you are not checking emails an hour before you go to bed, or not reading your emails until you've had your morning coffee, the important point is that you are in control. You've decided when it is best for you so you can be productive and focused. The feeling of being in control, not at the beck and whim of your demanding boss or your smartphone, is psychologically important. Prison is a punishment because it takes away people's freedom, control and decisions. You don't need to be a prisoner of unspoken work rules or a slave to technology.

The phrase "work smarter not harder" is so trite that I have avoided saying it up until now. What does it really mean to work smarter? Productivity in the industrial factory era was all about how fast you could do something. Now we work with knowledge. Our work is about analysing, understanding, thinking and creating ideas. We need to be persuasive and diplomatic with customers and colleagues. Our impact at work doesn't increase by working longer hours but by being more focused and more engaged in what we are doing. When we are focused and engaged we can manage a difficult conversation, or plan a way through a complex issue, or come up with a creative idea.

To be more focused, we should set the right conditions. In a world of distraction, with masses of information pouring through the internet, emails pinging and social media tweeting, it is hard to maintain attention. But we can learn and adapt our situation, so that we can concentrate and focus for intense and short periods of time. Then we get things done more effectively and get out of the office earlier. Imagine if you just had an extra half an hour a day – what other things you could get done in your life!

To be more engaged means first being at an optimal stress level – not bored or burned out. It means managing your mindset and energy levels so you can perform optimally. It's about being intrinsically motivated in what you're doing, having a clear purpose and reason for why you do what you do, having clear expectations and goals with steps of progress along the way. It may even mean getting into a sense of flow and being very engaged in your work.

And when you are not working, then it is time to switch off from work, physically and psychologically, and enjoy life. Most people in "knowledge" jobs are work-life integrators. Work crosses over to their private sphere and their non-work life crosses into their work sphere. Typically, with more career-focused people, their work life starts crossing over more often into their non-work life. Keeping the two separated can give more off-time to re-charge and re-energise. Then, with this energy and focus, you will be more productive when you are working.

Any of the tips in this book require you, and maybe the people around you, to change. If you want to work more productively then you can't keep doing things the same way. Start with a few small changes and take them step by step. Physically, you can't start by running a marathon tomorrow if you haven't broken into a sweat for two years. Likewise, you won't find that you reframe your habitual thinking overnight if this is the way you've been thinking for years.

But you will change if you imagine a goal, take small steps and feel the progress.

It doesn't need to be massive changes in your job, career or life. Small changes like learning to control your stress levels, or setting aside 25 to 50 minutes to work intensely on a project without interruption can have a major impact. Perhaps there is a need for some bigger changes. There may become a point where you question your work environment, organisation or boss. Maybe you decide it is them not you that should change. Your opportunity to change these factors is limited, so it may be time for you to take a new direction.

Learn to focus while you are at work and get more done. With the time you have gained, learn to switch off from work and enjoy life.

 Tip 35: Learn to focus while you are at work and get more done. With the time you have gained, you can then switch off from work, get out and enjoy life.

APPENDIX

Chapter 2: Stress Self-Assessment

MY PERSONAL STRESS RESPONSE

Think back to the last time you were moderately stressed. Tick those symptoms you experienced. Identify those which occurred first? This is your early warning system.

STRESS RESPONSE	Symptoms	Early warning
PSYCHOLOGICAL		
Angry		
Anxious, apprehensive, frightened, worrying thoughts		
Ashamed, embarrassed		
Depressed or feeling low		
Guilty		
Jealous		
Mood swings		
Reduced self-esteem		
Feeling out of control		
Unable to concentrate		
Negative thoughts and images		
Images of being out of control		
Increased daydreaming		
Nightmares		
BEHAVIOURAL		
Passive behaviour		
Aggressive behaviour		
Irritability, snappiness		
Increased alcohol consumption		
Increased caffeine consumption		
Comfort eating		
Disturbed sleep patterns		
Withdrawal or sulking		
Clenched fists, banging table, tapping foot or hand		
Compulsive or impulsive behaviour eg checking rituals		
Poor time management		
Reduced work performance		
Increased absenteeism from work		
Eating/talking/walking fast		
PHYSICAL		
Dry mouth		
Clammy hands		
Frequent colds and infections		
Palpitations or racing heartbeat		
Breathlessness		
Tightness or pain in the chest		
Migraines or tension headaches		
Vague aches and pains		
Backache		
Indigestion		
Diarrhoea, constipation, irritable bowel syndrome		
Skin complaints or allergies		
Asthma attacks		

Stress Self-Assessment (Palmer and Cooper, 2007)[74]

Chapter 3: Apps to Learn and Practice Meditation

1. Buddhify from www.buddhify.com

2. Headspace from https://www.headspace.com/headspace-meditation-app

Chapter 3: Playlist of 10 Relaxing Songs

1. Marconi Union – *Weightless*

2. Airstream – *Electra*

3. Enya – *Watermark*

4. Coldplay – *Strawberry Swing*

5. Barcelona – *Please Don't Go*

6. Adele – *Someone Like You*

7. Mogawi – *Take me Somewhere Nice*

8. Dido – *Thank you*

9. Norah Jones – *I don't Know Why*

10. Fink – *Looking Too Closely*

Chapter 5: Test Your Smartphone Addiction

ARE YOU A SMARTPHONE ADDICT?	Completely disagree	Somewhat Disagree	Disagree	Neutral	Agree	Somewhat Agree	Completely Agree
SCORE							
QUESTION	1	2	3	4	5	6	7
I would feel uncomfortable without constant access to information through my smartphone.							
I would be annoyed if I could not look information up on my smartphone when I wanted to do so.							
Being unable to get the news (e.g. happenings, weather, etc.) on my smartphone would make me nervous.							
I would be annoyed if I could not use my smartphone and/or its capabilities when I wanted to do so.							
Running out of battery power in my smartphone would scare me.							
If I were to run out of credits or hit my monthly data limit, I would panic.							
If I did not have a data signal or could not connect to wifi, then I would constantly check to see if I had a signal or could find a wifi network.							
If I could not use my smartphone, I would be afraid of getting stranded somewhere.							
If I could not check my smartphone for a while, I would feel a desire to check it.							
If I did not have my smartphone with me ...							
I would feel anxious because I could not instantly communicate with my family and/or friends.							
I would be worried because my family and/or friends could not reach me.							
I would feel nervous because I would not be able to receive text messages and calls.							
I would be anxious because I could not keep in touch with my family and/or friends.							
I would be nervous because I would not know if someone had tried to get a hold of me.							
I would feel anxious because my constant connection to my family and friends would be broken.							
I would be nervous because I would be disconnected from my online identity.							
I would be uncomfortable because I could not stay up-to-date with social media and online networks.							
I would feel awkward because I could not check my notifications for updates from my connections and online networks.							
I would feel anxious because I could not check my email messages.							
I would feel weird because I would not know what to do.							
TOTAL OF COLUMN							
MULTIPLY	×1	×2	×3	×4	×5	×6	×7
TOTAL EACH COLUMN							
ADD FOR FINAL SCORE							

BELOW 30:	Not at all nomophobic. You have a very healthy relationship with your device and have no problem being separated from it.
31-60:	Mild nomophobia. You get a little antsy when you forget your phone at home for a day or get stuck somewhere without wifi, but the anxiety isn't too overwhelming.
61-100:	Moderate nomophobia. You're pretty attached to your device. You often check for updates while you're walking down the street or talking to a friend, and you often feel anxious when you're disconnected.
101-120:	Severe nomophobia. You can barely go for 60 seconds without checking your phone. It's the first thing you check in the morning and the last at night, and dominates most of your activities in between.

Smartphone Addiction (Yildirim and Correia, 2015)[75]

Chapter 7: Questions to Ask to Help Identify if a Job is Fit for Purpose

1. What makes you smile (activities, people, events, hobbies)?

2. What are your favourite things from the past?

3. In what activities do you lose track of time?

4. What makes you feel great about yourself?

5. Who inspires you? Why?

6. What are you naturally good at?

7. What do people ask you for help at?

8. If you had to teach something, what would it be?

9. What would you regret not doing, being or having in life?

10. What causes do you strongly believe in?

Try thinking about:

1. What I am good at.

2. What I enjoy doing.

3. What gives me a sense of purpose.

Write down everything that comes to mind.

Chapter 7: Questions to Ask in an Interview to Assess the Work Culture

1. How do you measure performance of your employees? If the answer is a fair process based on actual achievements (outputs) rather than based on attendance time, then that is a good sign.

2. How do other people in the team integrate their work/life? The answer should tell you about working from home, flexitime and other policies.

3. What do you do to build good working relationships in the team? The answer can be about practical strategies e.g. team meetings, setting a common goal etc, or it could be about social activities, team-building events.

4. Why do you enjoy working here? The answer should be around the purpose and vision of what they see they can contribute to the organisation and greater world good, but less so to themselves.

5. How would you describe your management style? Of course, no one will say they are a toxic boss, but their answer can give you an idea if they focus more on people, process or tasks or a healthy mix of all three.

6. What do you see as the core purpose of this organisation? The answer should align with your values.

Endnotes

Introduction: Fast Forward

1   Poll conducted by European Agency for Safety and Health at Work downloaded from https://osha.europa.eu/en/themes/psychosocial-risks-and-stress

2   The first iPhone was released on 29 June 2007 and the first app with opening of the App Store on July 10, 2008 from https://en.wikipedia.org/wiki/History_of_iPhone

3   Research from the Radicati Group, Inc. and independent market research firm who have been tracking email usage since 1993. In 2009 each person sent and received 167 emails per day, increased by 30% to 215 emails in 2015.

4   Science Daily (2013) Science News downloaded from https://www.sciencedaily.com/releases/2013/05/130522085217.htm

5   Equilar blog (2016) CEO *tenure has increased nearly one full year since 2005*. Downloaded from http://www.equilar.com/blogs/59-ceo-tenure.html

6   Begey, S (2010) The Science of Aging Brains downloaded from *Newsweek* http://www.newsweek.com/science-aging-brains-73219

7   Jabr, F. (2011) *Cache Cab: Taxi Drivers' Brains Grow to Navigate London's Streets.* Scientific American downloaded from https://www.scientificamerican.com/article/london-taxi-memory/

Chapter 1: Mind Games: Beware of the Sabre-Toothed Tiger

8   Torres, N. (2015) *Just Hearing Your Phone Buzz Hurts Your Productivity.* Harvard Business Review downloaded from https://hbr.org/2015/07/just-hearing-your-phone-buzz-hurts-your-productivity

9   Sullivan, B. (2013) *Brain, Interrupted* The New York Times downloaded from http://www.nytimes.com/2013/05/05/opinion/sunday/a-focus-on-distraction.html

10   For a 12-hour recording of white noise https://www.youtube.com/watch?v=1KaOrSuWZeM

11   Reynolds, M (2017) *Desk traffic lights show when you're too busy for interruptions* downloaded from https://www.newscientist.com/article/2129342-desk-traffic-lights-show-when-youre-too-busy-for-interruptions/

12   There are two main challenges with most studies purporting to show difference between gender in multitasking. One is they are typically with a small sample size, secondly there is no commonly accepted test of multitasking, so the tasks the person is asked to do are not similar to what is required to be done in a job. http://www.spring.org.uk/2013/04/are-men-or-women-better-at-multitasking.php

13   Maybin, S (2017) *Busting the attention span myth*, BBC News downloaded from http://www.bbc.com/news/health-38896790

14   Bradberry, T (2017) *We're all used to an 8-hour work day. But is it effective?* Downloaded from https://www.weforum.org/agenda/2017/05/your-8-hour-day-isnt-working-heres-why

15   Downloaded from https://en.wikipedia.org/wiki/Alex_Mullen_(memory_athlete)

Chapter 2: Stress Makes You Stupid

16   Herbert, J (2016) *How Stress Can Damage the Brain*, Psychology Today downloaded from https://www.psychologytoday.com/blog/hormones-and-the-brain/201602/how-stress-can-damage-the-brain

17   Stress Hormones and Memory downloaded from http://www.humanstress.ca/stress/effects-of-stress-on-memory/stress-hormones-and-memory.html

18   Palmer, S & Cooper C (2007) *How to Deal with Stress*: Kogan Page, UK

19   Schaufeli, W., Leiter, M. & Maslach, C (2009) *Burnout: 35 years of Research and Practice*. Career Development International, 14 (3), 204-220.

20   Schaufeli, W., Leiter, M & Maslach, C. (2008) Burnout: 35 years of research and practice. *Career Development International*, 14 (3).

21   Middlemass, n. (2016) *Could bore-out be the next burn-out* HRD downloaded from http://www.hrmonline.ca/hr-news/could-boreout-be-the-next-burnout-206685.aspx

22   Burnett, D. (2016) *The Idiot Brain*. Guardian Faber

23   Luethi, M., Meier, B. & Sandi, C. (2008) Stress Effects on Working Memory, Explicit Memory and Implicit Memory for Neutral and Emotional Stimuli in Healthy Men, *Frontiers in Behavioral Neuroscience*, 2.

24   Klemm, W (2016) *Thwart Stress Effects of Memory*. Psychology Today downloaded from https://www.psychologytoday.com/blog/memory-medic/201612/thwart-stress-effects-memory

25   Pichon, S., Gelder, B. & Grezes, J (2012) *Threat Prompt Defensive Brain Response Independently of Attentional Control*, Cereb Cortex, 22 (2) 274-285

Chapter 3: Stress Less

26   Michelon P. (2010) Fitter bodies = fitter brains. True at all ages? Downloaded from http://sharpbrains.com/blog/2010/10/04/fitter-bodies-fitter-brains-true-at-all-ages/

27   Reynolds, G. (2012) *How Exercise Can Jog the Memory* The New York Times downloaded from http://well.blogs.nytimes.com/2012/05/30/how-exercise-can-jog-the-memory/

28   Mitchell, M (2009) *Physical activity may strengthen children's ability to pay attention* downloaded from https://news.illinois.edu/blog/view/6367/205988

29   Culpan V & Russel A (2016) *The Wake-Up Call: The importance of sleep in organisational life*. Ashridge Business School.

30   Jones, J (2013) *In U.S., 40% Get Less Than Recommended Amount of Sleep*. Gallup downloaded from http://www.gallup.com/poll/166553/less-recommended-amount-sleep.aspx

31   The Sleep Council (2013) *The Great British Bedtime Report* downloaded from https://www.sleepcouncil.org.uk/wp-content/uploads/2013/02/The-Great-British-Bedtime-Report.pdf

32   The Sleep Health Foundation downloaded from http://www.sleephealthfoundation.org.au/media-centre/media-releases/130-time-to-stop-dying-from-lack-of-sleep-australia-s-sleepiness-epidemic.html

33   Ma, A (2016) *A Sad Number of Americans Sleep with their Smartphone in their Hand*. Huffington Post downloaded from: http://www.huffingtonpost.com/2015/06/29/smartphone-behavior-2015_n_7690448.html

34   Schmerler, J (2015) *Why is Blue Light Before Bedtime Bad for Sleep?* Scientific American downloaded from https://www.scientificamerican.com/article/q-a-why-is-blue-light-before-bedtime-bad-for-sleep/

35   Interestingly *The Guinness Book of Records* stopped collecting records on how long a person could go without sleep as they believed it was too dangerous to people's health.

36   Vince, G (2005) *Coffee's effect revealed in brain scans*. New Scientist downloaded from https://www.newscientist.com/article/dn8401-coffees-effects-revealed-in-brain-scans/

37   Hendrickson, K. (2014) *Effects of a Sugar Overdose* downloaded from http://www.livestrong.com/article/242637-side-effects-of-a-sugar-overdose/

38   Poitras, C. (2012) *Even Mild Dehydration Can Alter Mood* downloaded from http://today.uconn.edu/2012/02/even-mild-dehydration-can-alter-mood/

39   Killingsworth, M. & Gilbert, D. (2010) *A Wandering Mind is an Unhappy Mind*. Science, Vol 330.

40   Zanesco, A., King, B., MacLean, K., Jacobs, T., Aichele, S., Wallace, B., Smallwood, J., Schooler, J. & Saron, C. (2016) *Meditation Training Influences Mind Wandering and Mindless Reading.* Psychology of Consciousness: Theory, Research and Practice, 3 (1), pp12-33.

41   Tang, Y., Yinghau, M., Wang, J., Fan, Y. Feng, S., Lu, Q., Yu, Q, Sui, D., Rothbart, M., Fan, M. & Posner, M. (2007) *Short-term meditation training improves attention and self-regulation.* Proceedings of the National Academy of Sciences of the USA, 104 (43).

42   Brown, K., Ryan, R. & Creswell, J. (2007) *Mindfulness: Theoretical Foundations and Evidence for its Salutary Effects.* Psychological Inquiry. Vol 18 (4), pp211-237.

43   Moore, A & Malinowski, P. (2009) *Meditation, Mindfulness and Cognitive Flexibility.* Consciousness and Cognition, 18, pp176-186.

44   Brown, K., Ryan, R. & Creswell, J. (2007) *Mindfulness: Theoretical Foundations and Evidence for its Salutary Effects.* Psychological Inquiry. Vol 18 (4), pp211-237.

45   Fox, J & Embry, E (1972) Music - an aid to productivity. *Applied Ergonomics*, 3 (4), pp202-205.

46   Kuepper-Tetzel, C. (2016) *Listening to Music while Studying: A good or a Bad Idea?* Downloaded from http://www.learningscientists.org/blog/2016/11/10-1

47   The Black Eyed Peas – *I Gotta Feeling* https://www.youtube.com/watch?v=uSD4vsh1zDA

48   Enya – *Waterfall* https://www.youtube.com/watch?v=xf8-KtfDcAY

49   TED Talk: How to make stress your friend.   Kelly McGonigal.   https://www.ted.com/talks/kelly_mcgonigal_how_to_make_stress_your_friend?language=en

Chapter 4: Get the Right Mindset and Get More Done

50   Grant, A., (2008) *Employees without a Cause: The Motivational Effects of Prosocial Impact in Public Service.* International Public Management Journal, 11 (1).

51   Ariely, D., Kamenica, E. & Prelec, D. (2008) *Man's Search for Meaning: The Case of Legos.* Journal of Economic Behavior & Organization, 67 (3-4), pp671-677.

52   Teresa Amabile (2013) *Slowing the Work Treadmill.* Harvard Gazette downloaded from http://news.harvard.edu/gazette/story/2013/08/slowing-the-work-treadmill/

53   Lyubomirsky, S., King, L. & Diener, E. (2005) *The Benefits of Frequent Positive Affect: Does Happiness Lead to Success?* American Psychological Association, 131 (6) 803-855.

54   Chancellor, J., Layous, K. & Lyubomirsky, S. (2015) *Recalling Positive Events at Work Makes Employees Feel Happier, Move More, but Interact Less: A 6-Week Randomized Controlled Intervention at a Japanese Workplace.* Journal of Happiness Studies (16) 871

Chapter 5: Build a Wall Around Your Castle

55   Deloitte (2016) *Global Mobile Consumer Survey* 2016 UK Cut downloaded from https://www.deloitte.co.uk/mobileuk/better-living/

56   Beall, A., (2016) *Now that TEXT appeal.* Mail Online downloaded from http://www.dailymail.co.uk/sciencetech/article-3594526/Now-s-TEXT-appeal-One-ten-people-admit-look-phone-sex.html

57   Kossek, E., (2016) *Managing Work-life Boundaries in the Digital Age.* Organizational Dynamics, 45, pp258-270.

58   Webb, C., (2016) *How to Have a Good Day.* Crown Business: UK

Chapter 6: Change and Making It Stick

59   Luciani, J., (2015) *Why 80 percent of New Year's Resolutions Fail* downloaded from http://health.usnews.com/health-news/blogs/eat-run/articles/2015-12-29/why-80-percent-of-new-years-resolutions-fail

60   Tim Urban: Wait but Why Blog *Why Procrastinators Procrastinate* downloaded from https://waitbutwhy.com/2013/10/why-procrastinators-procrastinate.html

61   Tim Urban's Ted Talk *Inside the Mind of a Master Procrastinator* https://www.ted.com/talks/tim_urban_inside_the_mind_of_a_master_procrastinator

62   Psychology Today *Procrastination: Ten Things to Know*, downloaded from https://www.psychologytoday.com/articles/200308/procrastination-ten-things-know

63   Palmer, S., & Cooper C., (2007) *How to Deal with Stress*: Kogan Page, UK

64   Duhigg, C., (2012) *The Power of Habit: Why We Do What We Do and How to Change.* Random House: UK

65   Amabile, T. & Kramer, S. (2011) *The Progress Principle.* Harvard Business Review Press, Boston.

66   Neenan, M & Dryden W. (2014*) Life Coaching: A cognitive Behavioural Approach.* Routledge: London

Chapter 7: Crazy Cultures and Toxic Workplaces

67   Bellezza, S., Paharia N. & Keinan, A. (2016) *Research: Why Americans Are So Impressed by Busyness. Harvard Business Review* downloaded from https://hbr.org/2016/12/research-why-americans-are-so-impressed-by-busyness

68   *The Workplace Employee Relations Survey* (2011) downloaded from https://www.gov.uk/government/uploads/system/uploads/attachment_data/file/336651/bis-14-1008-WERS-first-findings-report-fourth-edition-july-2014.pdf

69   HR Magazine (2016) *Over-ambitious Workers make Others Insecure* downloaded from http://www.hrmagazine.co.uk/article-details/over-ambitious-workers-make-colleagues-insecure-about-their-performance

70   Rozovsky, J., (2015) *The five keys to a successful Google Team* downloaded from https://rework.withgoogle.com/blog/five-keys-to-a-successful-google-team/

71   Porath, C., (2017) *How Rudeness Stops People from Working Together* Harvard Business Review downloaded from https://hbr.org/2017/01/how-rudeness-stops-people-from-working-together

72   Hathaway, B., (2016) *Do the math - why some people are jerks yet others are even nice to strangers* downloaded from https://phys.org/news/2016-01-mathwhy-people-jerks-nice-strangers.html

73   Hurst, A., (2014) *The Purpose Economy*: Elevate: USA

Appendix

74   Palmer, S., & Cooper C., (2007) *How to Deal with Stress*: Kogan Page, UK

75   Yildirim, C., & Correia, A., (2015) Exploring the dimensions of nomophobia: Development and validation of a self-reported questionnaire. *Computers in Human Behavior*, 49, August, pp130-137

About the Author

Jane Piper is an Organisational Psychologist who grew up in New Zealand. She has been living abroad for many years, most recently for over 10 years in Switzerland. Bringing a unique blend of kiwi creativity and Swiss efficiency, she combines writing, consulting and coaching on topics of careers, collaboration and culture.

With twenty years' experience in various corporations, she is a keen observer of people, careers and organisational culture, often seeing the irony and humour. She believes that work should be an enjoyable experience with opportunities for people to grow and learn. She advises people how to find fulfilling and enjoyable work, and organisations how to make their work practices and culture more human-centric.